GATESHEAD
THROUGH TIME
Nick Neave

AMBERLEY PUBLISHING

Acknowledgements

The author would like to express his thanks to the following individuals and organisations that have contributed to this book:

The Committee and members of Sunniside & District History Society; Anthea Lang, Local History & Heritage Manager, Gateshead City Council; Eric Briggs, owner of *Station Stamp Shop* on Coatsworth Road whose advice has been invaluable; Keith Lant who assisted me in locating many of the sites featured in this book; Julian Harrop from Beamish Museum Ltd; Annette Morton from Power League, Gateshead; the members of the Facebook group 'Gateshead Local History', especially Connie Wilson, Michael Paul Allen, George Tullin and Susan Sherriff who have been most helpful.

Ownership of the photographs is as follows:
All of the 'new' photographs (except for the picture of Gateshead FC on page 56) were taken by the author during March 2010 and so copyright for these images resides with Sunniside & District History Society. Jeff Heads of '*DigitaLab*' (please visit his website at http://www.theviewfinder.co.uk) kindly allowed me to use his excellent photograph of the Great North Run on page 7.
Gateshead Council have supplied the 'old' photographs on pages 6-7, 10-11, 14-16, 18, 20-24, 27, 30, 33-36, 39-43, 46-51, 53-54, 56-57, 60-61, 64-66, 71-75, 82-83, 85-88, 90-95.
The 'old' pictures on pages 8 and 9 have been donated by Michael Paul Allen.
Copyright for the images on pages 52, 58 and 59 resides with Trevor Ermel.
Beamish Museum Ltd provided the images on pages 5, 12, 13, and 96.
Sunniside & District History Society Photographic Archive supplied the images on pages 17, 19, 25, 28-29, 31, 37-38, 44-45, 62-63, 67-70, 76-81, 84, 89.
Susan Sheriff supplied the picture of the Roundhouse on page 26.
Ian Ayris from Newcastle City Council kindly gave permission for me to use the picture on page 32.
The image of Redheugh Park on page 55 was kindly supplied by Ernie Curry, historian for Gateshead FC.
Mike Coulson from Gateshead FC provided the recent photograph of Gateshead FC on page 56.

First published 2010

Amberley Publishing Plc
Cirencester Road, Chalford,
Stroud, Gloucestershire, GL6 8PE

www.amberley-books.com

Copyright © Nick Neave, 2010

The right of Nick Neave to be identified as the Author of this work has been asserted in accordance with the Copyrights, Designs and Patents Act 1988.

ISBN 978 1 84868 272 6

British Library Cataloguing in Publication Data.
A catalogue record for this book is available from the British Library.

Typeset in 9.5pt on 12pt Celeste.
Typesetting by Amberley Publishing.
Printed in the UK.

Introduction

Samuel Johnson once described Gateshead as 'a dirty lane leading to Newcastle' and unfortunately such an image has long persisted. It is often assumed by visitors to the area that Gateshead is an offshoot to Newcastle, created by Newcastle spreading south of the river. This is not the case. Gateshead has long been an industrial and urban centre in its own right, with a proud history, and a rich heritage. Gateshead is first mentioned in Bede's *History of the English Church and People* and the first settlements lay along the river Tyne close to where the Tyne and Swing Bridges now stand. By 1344 coal-mining had become a significant feature of the area, and wharves were constructed along the river at Pipewellgate to transport the 'black gold'. Gateshead continued to develop in the 1600s but during and after the Civil War the town began to decline, as it was no longer economical to mine the deeper coal seams further inland that were now all that remained of its coal riches. It was not until the mid 1700s that technological advances meant that such reserves could be exploited, and Gateshead once more began to prosper. Coal mining led to ship building which in turn led to rope-making; other important industries consisted of mills, quarries, potteries, ironworks, brickworks and chemical works.

The cumulative effect of this industrial development was to create a dramatic increase in the population, and by the 1800s citizens were packed into poor insanitary housing that bred a host of social and health problems; outbreaks of cholera for example being distressingly common. By the 1860s, more land to the south and east became available for public housing and so Gateshead gradually spread from its original heart. Communities were established at Low Fell and Sheriff Hill and Saltwell Park was created for public benefit in 1877. Imposing residences were constructed for the well-to-do industrialists who had triggered Gateshead's expansion, and the Housing Act of 1909 led to the clearance of some of the overcrowded slum areas. After the

First World War other areas of poor housing were demolished and new communities established in Carr Hill, Wrekenton, Deckham and Lobley Hill, with the construction of the Tyne Bridge in the 1920s the slums of Pipewellgate and Bottle Bank were finally cleared.

From the 1920s Gateshead began a slow industrial decline as the traditional heavy industries began to fail, and an attempt was made to improve matters with the creation of the Team Valley Trading Estate in the 1930s. During the 1950s, attempts to solve the chronic housing shortage led to the construction of tower blocks, and 'village' concepts, though they generally led to a collapse of the community spirit and greater social problems. During the 1960s and 1970s the old heart of Gateshead was largely cleared to provide relief roads, flyovers and bypasses that seemed only to exist to enable people to reach Newcastle with greater ease, leaving Gateshead even more isolated and resentful.

From such bad times Gateshead has experienced a slow regeneration, not only of its landscape but also of its pride. The building of the Metro Centre in 1986 and the National Garden Festival in 1990 kick-started further civic and social developments and more recent high-profile developments along the quayside such as the Millennium Bridge, the Baltic and the Sage and the sculpture the 'Angel of the North' have further led to a rise in civic pride.

The folk of Gateshead have endured years of boom and bust and their town has undergone many dramatic transformations. By putting together old and new photographs the reader may come to appreciate the extent of such changes and how they have influenced the citizens of Gateshead. What is clear from comparing the old and new images is that while some parts of Gateshead have experienced significant regeneration, some elements remain virtually unchanged. It is also clear that some of the regeneration may have been in the 'name of progress' but it has not exactly led to an improvement in the environment.

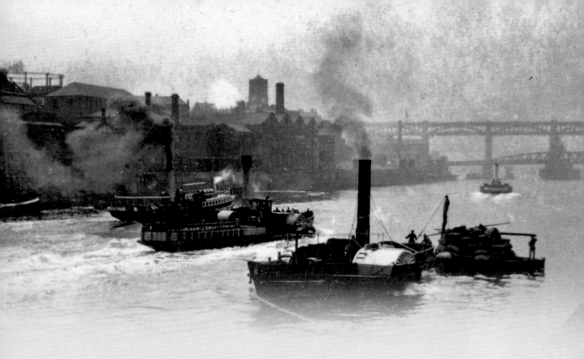

CHAPTER 1

Around the River

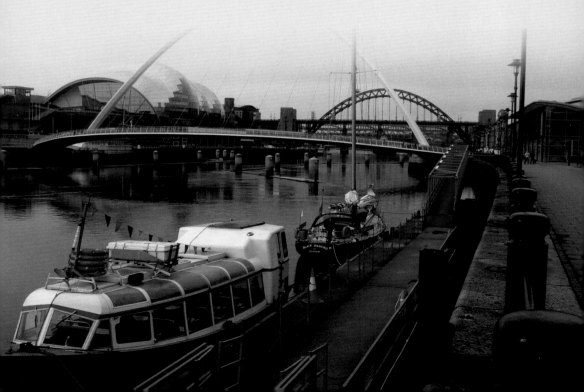

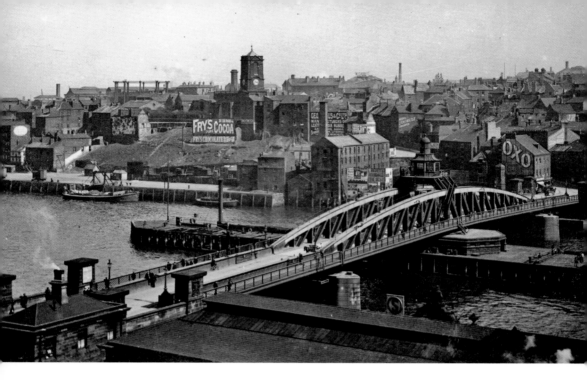

The Swing Bridge

The road to Gateshead pictured sometime between 1888-1925. The bridge was designed by William Armstrong and opened in 1876. St Mary's Church can clearly be seen dominating the river bank. In the same view today, St Mary's is almost hidden behind the Tyne Bridge (completed in 1928), and is overshadowed by the Tyne Bridge Tower. The Hilton Hotel replaces the long-demolished older buildings. The building that lies directly in front of the Swing Bridge is Neptune House built in 1888, now a nightclub called 'Sea'.

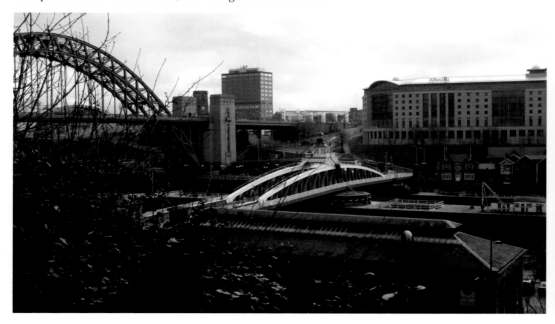

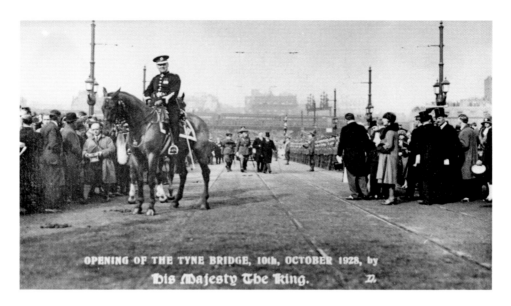

OPENING OF THE TYNE BRIDGE, 10th, OCTOBER 1928, by
His Majesty The King.

Bridging the Gap

Construction began in August 1925 and Dorman Long and Co. of Middlesbrough completed the bridge on 25 February, 1928. The opening ceremony was held on the 10 October 1928, with King George V and Queen Mary leading the procession from Newcastle to Gateshead. The bridge is 162 metres long and stands 26 metres above the river. On the right can be seen All Saints' Church, completed in 1896. Every year at about the same time, over 50,000 runners surge over the bridge into Gateshead on their way to South Shields to complete the 'Great North Run'.

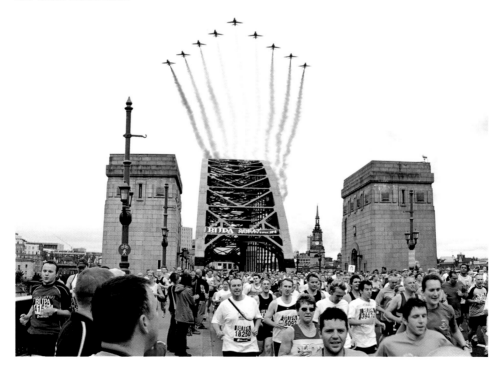

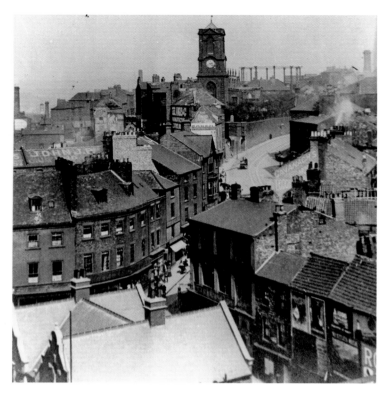

Around St. Mary's
The area around St
Mary's viewed from
the High Level Bridge
before the building
of the Tyne Bridge.
This was a thriving
economic and social
centre, but when the
construction of the
Tyne Bridge began in
1924 much of the area
surrounding St Mary's
was demolished, along
with the upper end
of the High Street,
Church Street, Bridge
Street and part of
Bottle Bank. In the new
picture, the buildings
in the bottom left hand
corner (and of course
St. Mary's) are all that
remain.

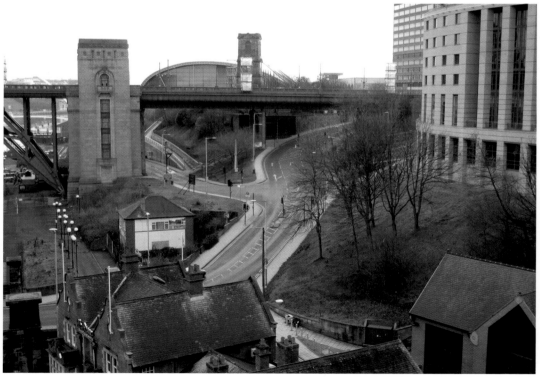

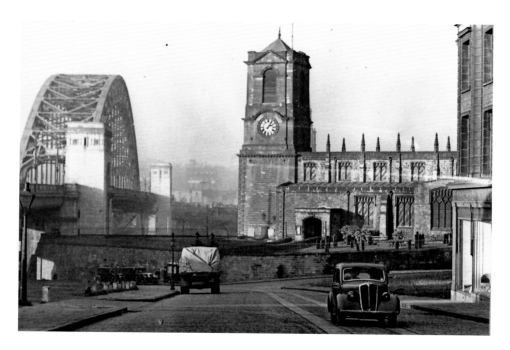

Two Icons

This image was taken in the late 1940s or early 1950s. The granite towers of the Tyne Bridge house lift shafts, though the lifts were never installed! The Church of St Mary the Virgin to give it its full title was built in the twelfth century, and until 1825 was the only church in Gateshead. The church was damaged by cannon balls during the English Civil War, and was severely damaged during the 'Great Fire' of 1854. It closed in the early 1980s, becoming an auction house in 1990 and was leased by Gateshead Council in 2000. Funding provided by the Heritage Lottery Fund enabled the Council to purchase the building outright and has recently been refurbished to become 'Gateshead Heritage @ St Mary's'.

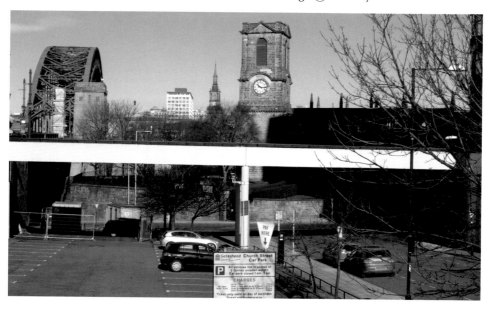

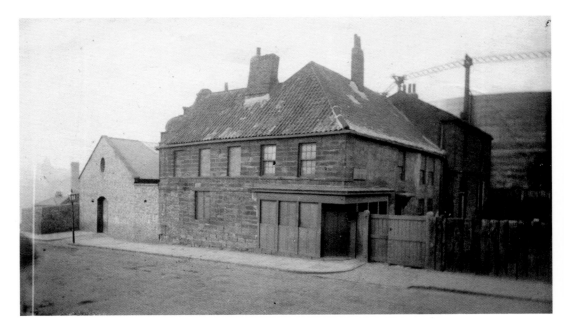

The Rectory

This is Oakwellgate Rectory pictured around 1836; it was the former rectory of St. Mary's, but soon became hemmed in by industrial development (note the gasometer in the background) and by 1839 the tenants had moved to Bensham. The building was then used as a public house (the Brandling Arms) and between 1861-1863 was the first Co-op store in Gateshead. It was mostly demolished in 1914 and the site is now occupied by the striking Sage, the £70 million music, education and performance centre which opened in 2004.

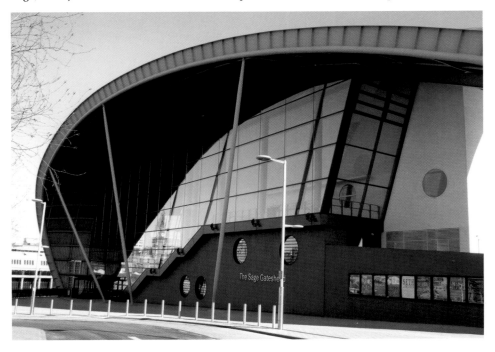

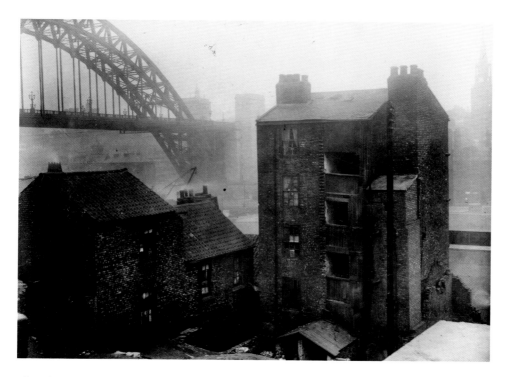

The Clearance Begins

The area surrounding St. Marys is called Oakwellgate, said to have been named after a well which was sheltered by an oak tree, though other sources note that the area had also been referred to as 'Aquelgate', with 'gate' being used in the sense of 'street' or 'lane'. This is a view of some of the buildings in Oakwellgate just before they were cleared in the 1930s. All Saints' Church is on the right in both pictures.

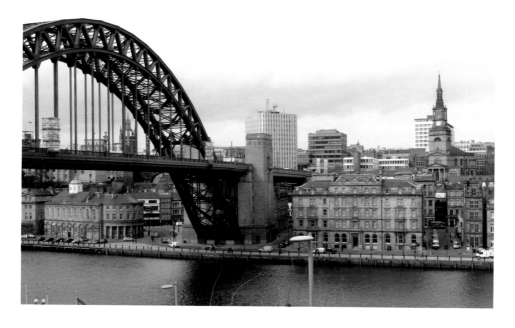

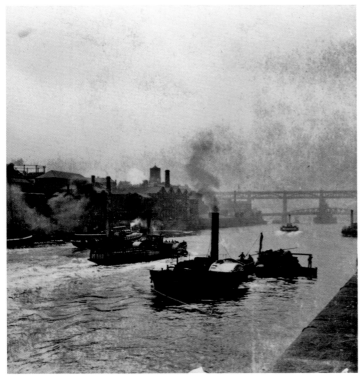

A Busy River

The river Tyne looking towards Gateshead *c.* 1915. St. Mary's can clearly be seen in the distance and the industrial development around Oakwellgate is obvious. It is also easy to see that at this time the river was a hive of activity, with various steam-powered vessels plying their trade. The High Level Bridge and Swing Bridge can be seen in the background. Today the industry is gone, and the few vessels are pleasure craft. The Millennium Bridge and Tyne Bridge obscure the High Level and Swing Bridge, St Mary's can just be seen to the right of the Sage.

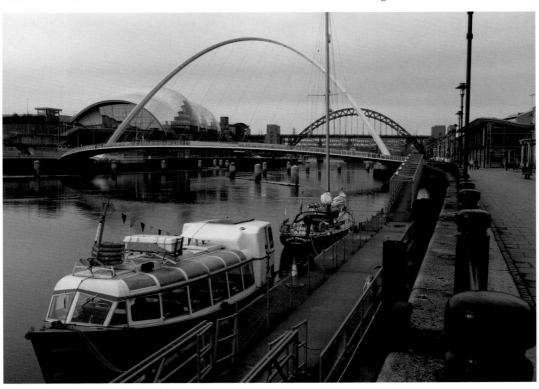

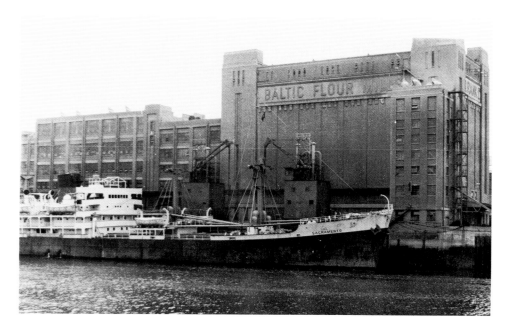

From Industry to Art

The Baltic Flour Mill was opened in 1950 and was built on land formerly occupied by Gateshead Iron Works. It was owned by Joseph Rank Ltd, and the company named all of their flour mills after the seas of the world which is why it came to have this unusual name. At its height it employed around 300 people, but production ceased in 1981, and its warehouses were demolished shortly after. In 1992 Gateshead Council proposed a plan to convert the empty building into an art gallery, but it was not until 1998 that the plan came to fruition. The Baltic Centre for Contemporary Art opened in July 2002 and has proved to be a popular, if controversial tourist attraction.

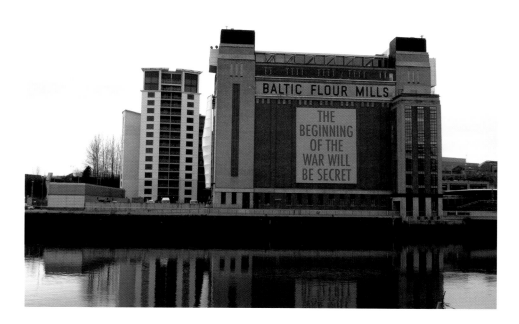

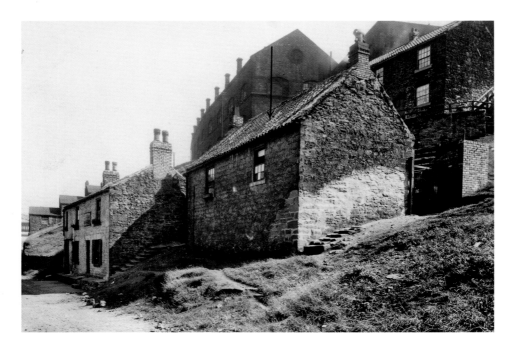

Pipewellgate

This notorious slum area ran parallel to the river Tyne from Redheugh to what is now the Swing Bridge. It was originally a separate township called 'pipe well' after a lane leading to the wooden pipes that carried water through the area. From the eighteenth century this area became associated with dense, overcrowded tenements and small factories and workshops. The area frequently experienced outbreaks of infectious diseases such as cholera. Few businesses remain and those pictured here are 'for sale'. The steep banks were landscaped in 1969-1970, and are now part of a sculpture park.

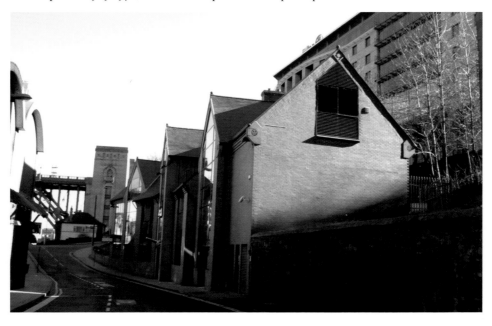

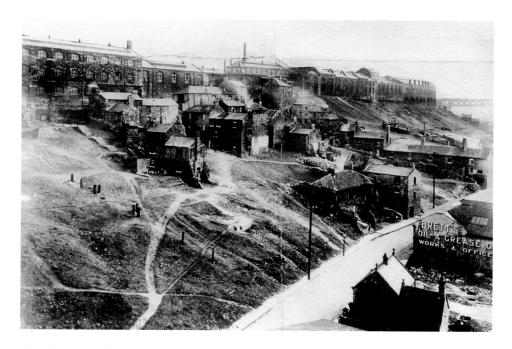

The Clearance Continues

Pipewellgate around 1935. The housing and industrial developments can clearly be seen perched on the steep banks, but it is in the process of being cleared. The map of 1894 reveals the extent of the industry here, with bottle works, grease works, manure works, chemical works, foundries and a paper mill being identified. During the clearances of the 1930s most of the area was demolished, leaving only a few buildings that were later converted into bars and restaurants. The sole industrial survivor is Brett's Oil and Grease Company, part of which is the white building to the right of the new picture.

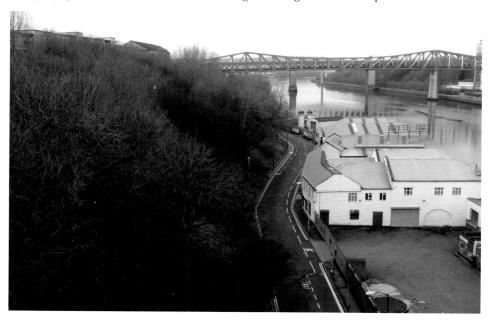

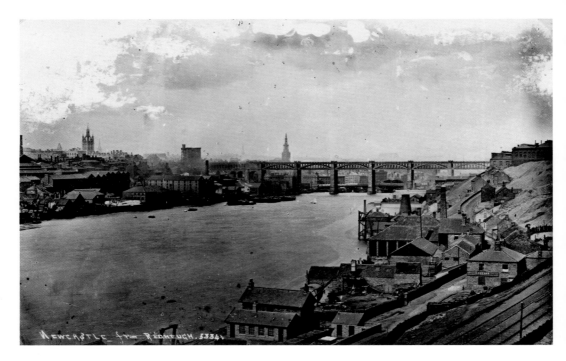

Redheugh

The view towards Newcastle from Redheugh. The High Level Bridge dominates the river. It was designed by Robert Stephenson and construction began in 1847, the formal opening taking place on 27 September 1849 by Queen Victoria. The bridge was closed for repairs in 2005 and did not open again until 2008. Other key landmarks (from left to right) are St. Nicholas, the Castle Keep and All Saints'. In the new picture all of the industry around Redheugh has vanished, the High Level Bridge is hidden behind the King Edward VII Bridge (1906) and the Queen Elizabeth II Metro Bridge (1981). The Newcastle landmarks can still be seen.

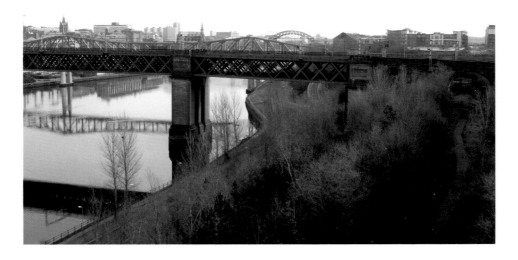

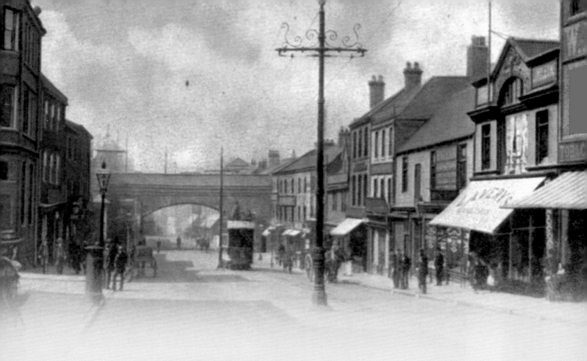

CHAPTER 2

Around the High Street

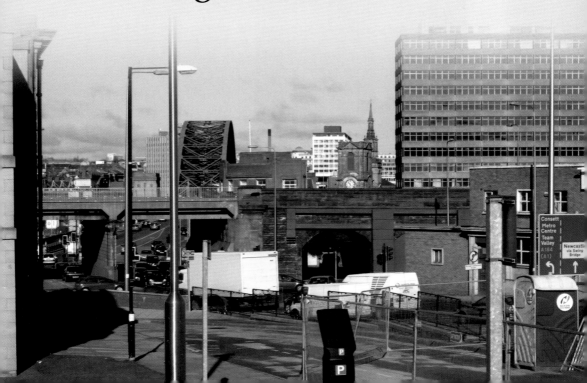

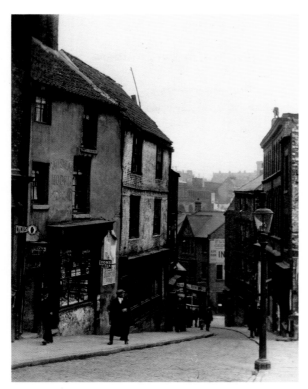

Bottle Bank

Looking down Bottle Bank towards Bridge Street, at the corner of Church Street. At this time this area formed the commercial and industrial heart of Gateshead, until the mass demolitions during the 1930s onwards. The name of this street is derived from the Saxon word 'botl' meaning 'settlement' or 'dwelling'. It was sometimes erroneously called 'Battle Bank'. Church Street was completed in 1790 in order to accommodate traffic travelling to and from the recently built Tyne Bridge. It was not named until 1826 and for many years was simply referred to as 'the New Street'. The Hilton Hotel, built in 2004 and Tyne Bridge approach roads have replaced most of this area.

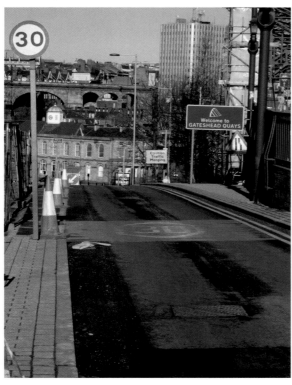

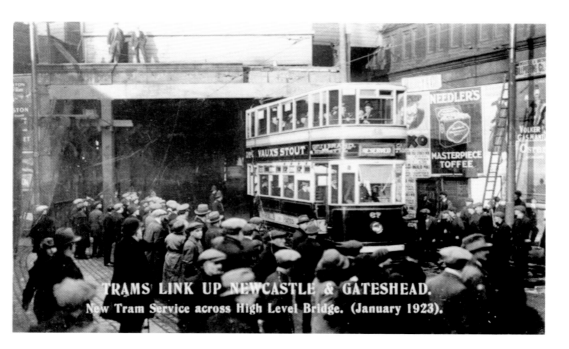

TRAMS LINK UP NEWCASTLE & GATESHEAD.
New Tram Service across High Level Bridge. (January 1923).

The Tram System is Connected

This photograph captures the moment in January 1923 when the first tram crossed the High Level Bridge onto Wellington Street to provide the first service between Newcastle and Gateshead. Gateshead Railway Station was once located to the right of this picture, but it closed in 1850 because the High Level Bridge and Newcastle's Central Station diverted the main rail travel directly to Newcastle. The station became a shed for repairing locomotives. This is still a major transport route, with the number 1 bus on its way to Kibblesworth.

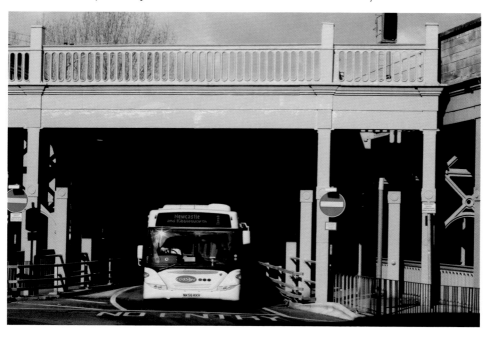

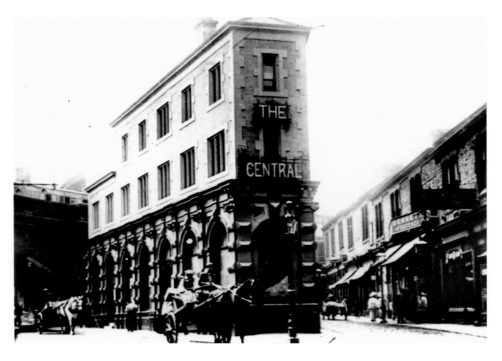

'The Coffin'

The Central pictured in the 1920s stands in Half Moon Lane, one of the few remaining areas of Victorian Gateshead. It is known as 'the coffin' by locals in reference to its distinctive shape constrained as it was by the railway line that runs behind it. It was built in 1854 to designs by Matthew Thompson for a local wine merchant, and retains much of its original Victorian character with façades of original fanlights and stained glass, and a panelled ceiling. The building is currently being renovated both inside and out and hopefully this distinctive old pub will soon be back to its former splendour.

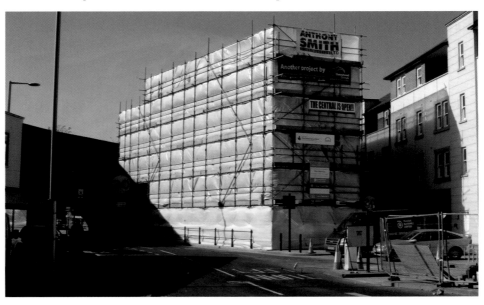

Get Carter!

The multi-storey car park and Trinity Square Shopping Centre viewed from the junction of Ellison Street and High Street during the 1970s. The centre was planned as a rival to Newcastle's Eldon Square and opened in 1967. The car park opened in 1969 and was hailed by architects as a classic of the 'Brutalist' style. It was supposed to include a small theatre and cinema, and a restaurant, but these were never built. It achieved notoriety by appearing in a key scene in the cult film *Get Carter* released in 1971. The car park is regarded by most locals as an eyesore and is currently being demolished. The horse presumably moved onto greener pastures long ago.

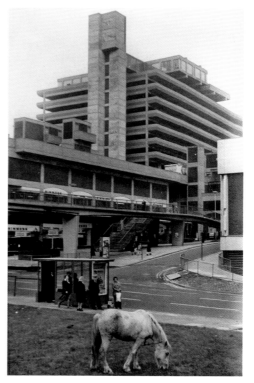

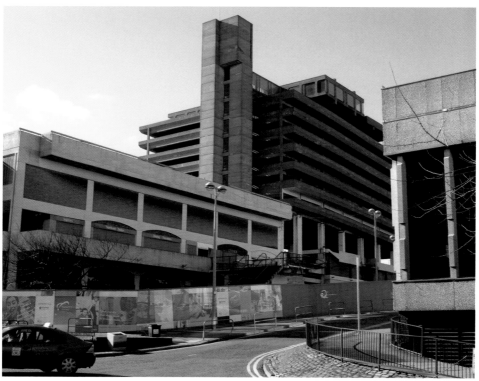

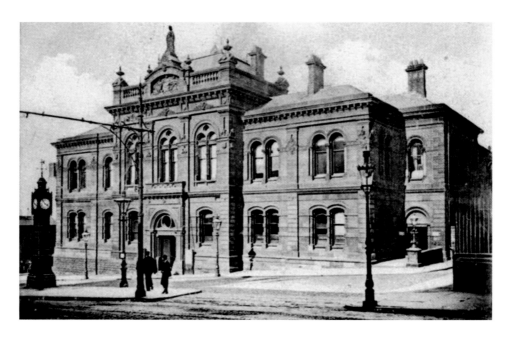

The 'New' Town Hall

In 1835 Gateshead Council was formed with George Hawks being elected as Mayor and William Kell being named as Town Clerk. For the first year the new Town Council met in the Anchorage public house, and then in St Mary's church. In 1836 a house was rented in Oakwellgate for the sole purpose of hosting the Council and the offices of the Police. A new Town Hall was built in 1844 but this had to be demolished in 1867 to make way for the railway extension to Team Valley. The Town Hall we see today was designed by John Johnstone (he also designed the former Gateshead Public Library just down the road) and it opened in June 1868. The statue on the parapet is that of Queen Victoria.

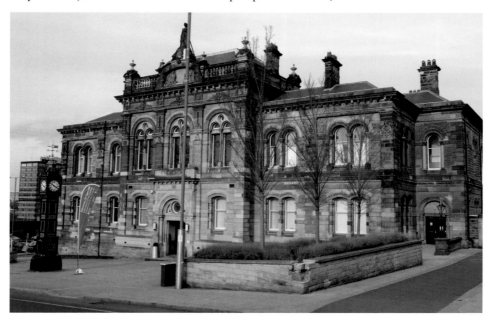

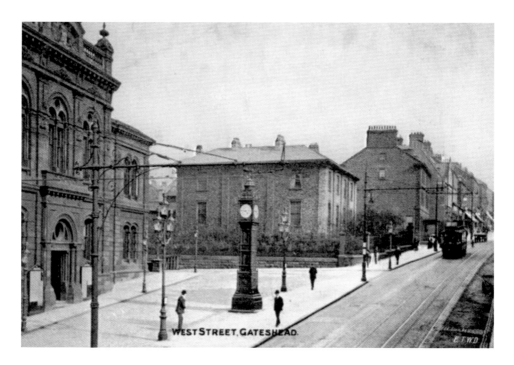

WEST STREET, GATESHEAD.

The Clock

Another view of the Town Hall looking south, as a tram descends the steep incline on West Street. A carving of a goat's head on the Town Hall may hint at the original name for Gateshead as the area was apparently noted for its numerous wild goats. However as a portcullis (gate) also appears on the town's coat of arms, the 'goat' interpretation is not conclusive. The clock tower in front of the Town Hall is cast iron and was built in 1892 by Gillett & Johnson of Croydon. The Council moved to the new Civic Centre on Regent Street in 1986, and the Town Hall has been used for numerous purposes, including hosting Newcastle's Tyneside Cinema during its recent refurbishment.

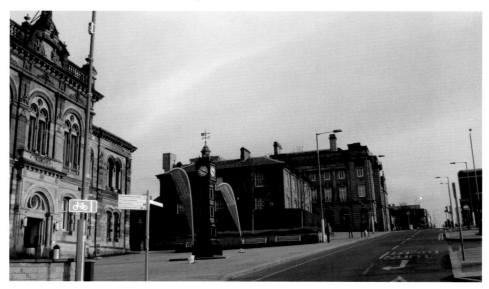

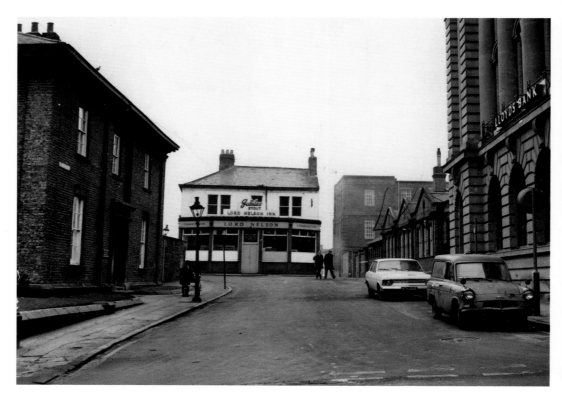

Time Gentlemen Please!

The Lord Nelson pub on Nelson Street photographed in 1969. The building on the left was constructed in the 1830s and in 1855 became the town dispensary; it remains in use as council offices. Lloyds Bank can be seen on the right in both pictures, and it remains a bank. The Lord Nelson and the building to the right of it have been demolished.

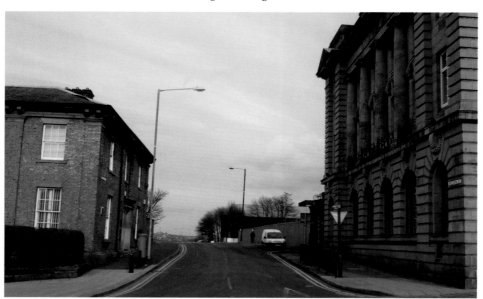

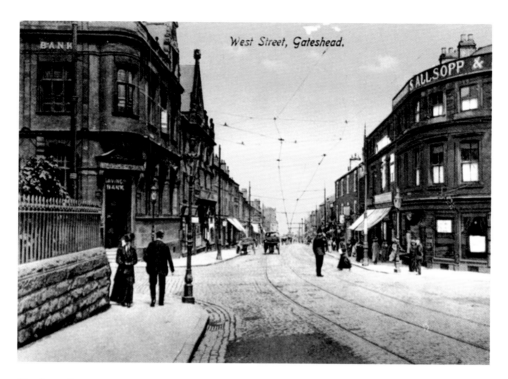

The Last Corner

Looking north along West Street. The railings of St. Joseph's Church are the only remnants of this scene. The church was completed in 1859 and was the first established Roman Catholic church in the town, being financed largely by public subscription. On the north-west corner an octagonal base can be seen, and it has been suggested that this was supposed to form the base of a tower or spire that was never built. In the background on the left in the recent picture is Gateshead Interchange.

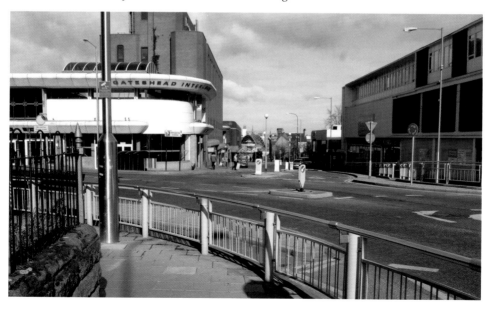

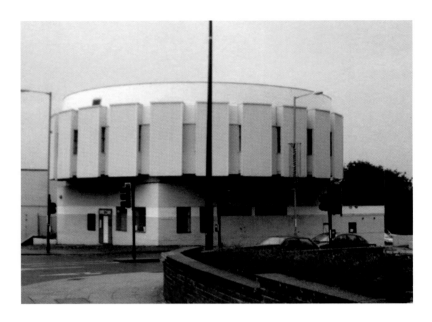

The Roundhouse

One of Gateshead's most distinctive buildings was the 'Roundhouse', on the corner of West Street and Charles Street. It was constructed in 1968 as a social club for the Boilermaker's Union. It was then purchased by local comedian Bobby Pattinson in 1978 and called 'The Talk of the Tyne'. It was later sold off and was purchased by Christian International Europe in 1999 as a base for their European operations, and as a place of worship for their local congregation. It was recently demolished and as yet nothing has taken its place.

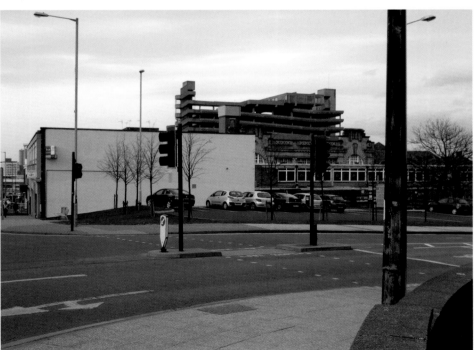

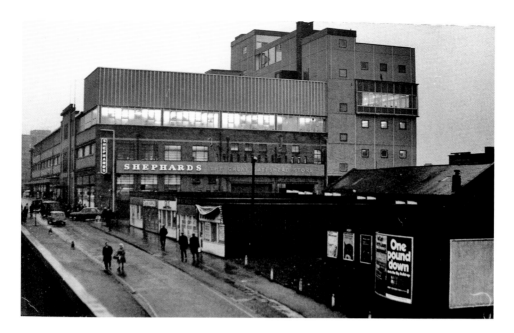

One Empire to Another

Shepard's of Ellison Street/West Street was one of several shops owned by Emerson Shephard. He began his empire in 1906 with a small shop in Swinburne Street that later transferred to West Street. Between 1908-1924 he opened further shops on Coatsworth Road, in Dunston, Whitley Bay, Ashington, Birtley and Hebburn. The West Street store was his largest, after an extension was built in 1934 it had three floors containing thirty departments covering a floorspace of around 100,000 square feet. The original building was destroyed by fire in 1946 but was rebuilt in 1949. In 1980 it became 'Shopping City' and closed in 1986. It was demolished, and is now the site of Tesco car park.

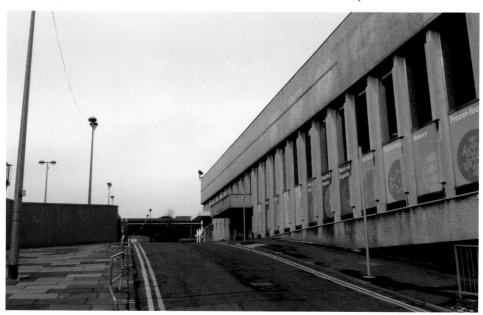

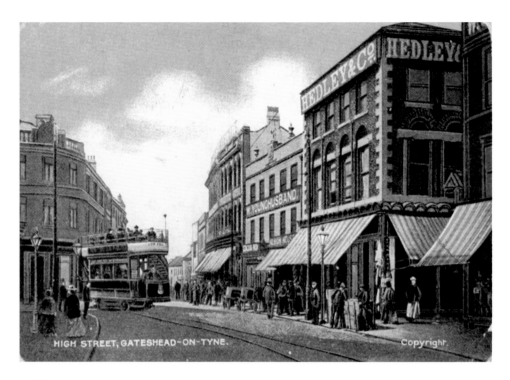

HIGH STREET, GATESHEAD-ON-TYNE.

Copyright

Half Moon Street

A view of the High Street with a tram turning into Half Moon Lane at the Half Moon Inn. Passengers would alight here for three main department stores: Snowball's (to the immediate right of the tram), Younghusband's and Hedley's. Snowball's was founded by William Snowball and opened in 1850, it began as a draper's, but expanded into other wares and soon became very successful. By 1889 it employed over 200 staff. It closed in the 1940s. This section of the High Street was demolished for the Tyne Bridge approach road, though Half Moon Lane can still be seen in the recent photograph.

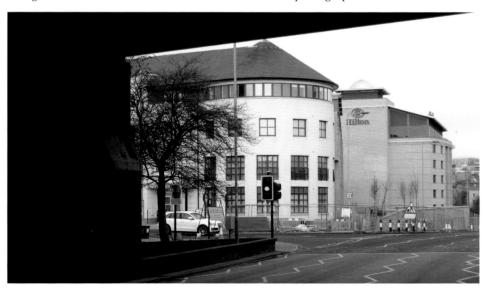

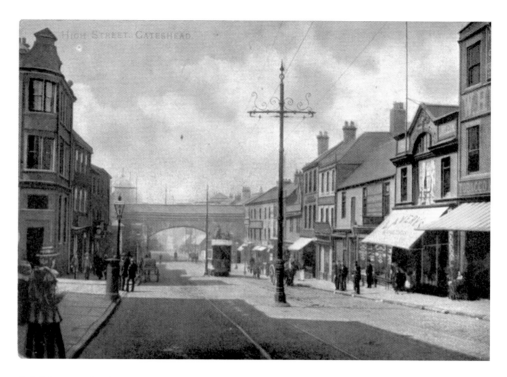

A Bridge too Far?

Gateshead High Street, looking north towards the railway bridge, *c.* 1905. The road behind the post box is Swinburne Street. Shops had been established on the High Street since the 1700s, and a wide variety of trades and businesses were represented. In 1835 it was described as the town's '...only one good and wide street'. Swinburne Street still exists though everything else has changed.

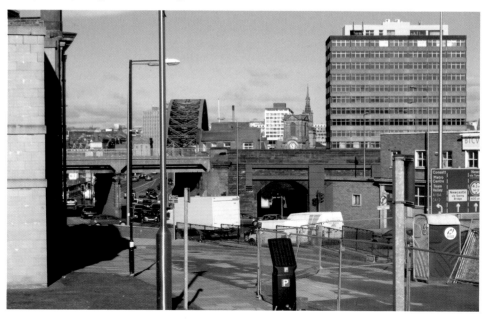

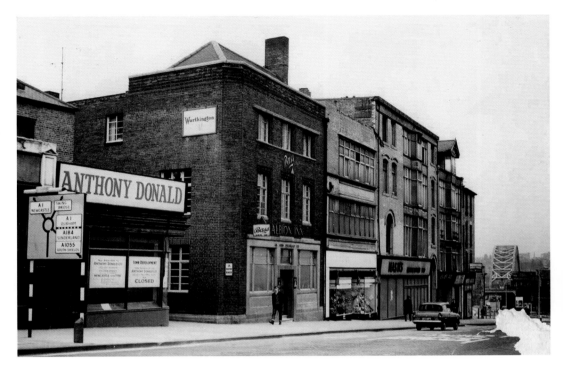

The March of Progress?

The High Street photographed around 1965. The second building from the left is the Albion Inn public house situated at number 148. This area was redeveloped during the 1960s and 1970s to improve access to the Tyne Bridge, which can just be seen in the background, and the Albion was consigned to history. Tesco now occupies this site.

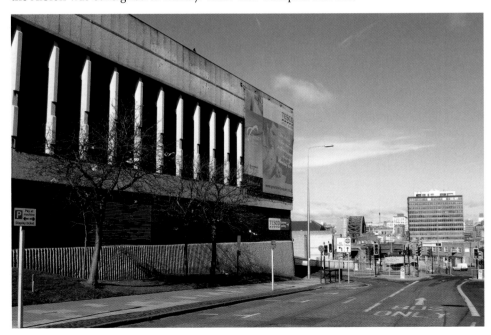

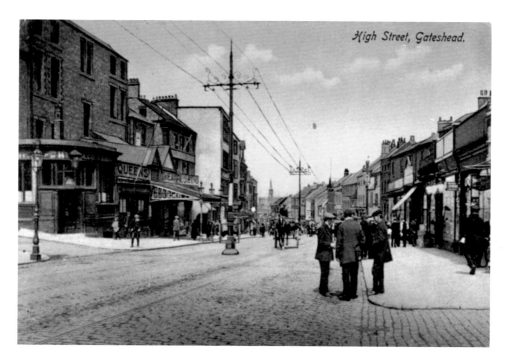

High Street, Gateshead.

The End of an Era

The High Street looking north in the early 1900s. Today, Tesco occupies the site where the Queen's Theatre once stood just after the corner of Ellison Street. The theatre had a varied history, being in turn a Wesleyan Methodist Chapel (1815), United Methodist Free Church Chapel (1861), Hall of Varieties (1882), boxing hall, Salvation Army hall, theatre (Theatre Royal – 1887, Queen's Theatre – 1894, New Hippodrome – 1916) and finally a cinema (The Queen – 1919) before eventually closing in 1923. To the left of the Theatre is the Ellison Arms. Ellison Street can still be seen on the left of the recent photograph but everything else has vanished.

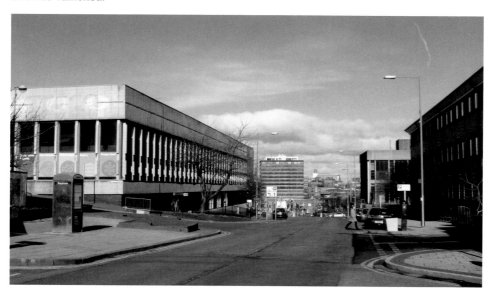

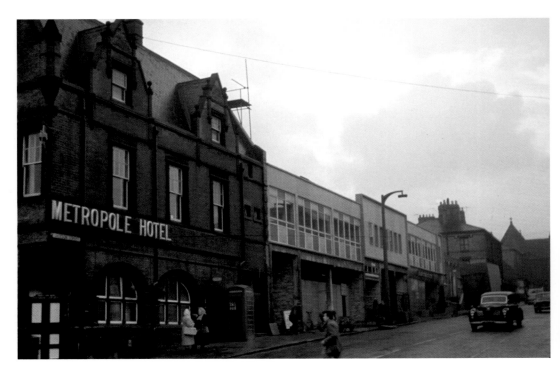

A Good Night Out

The imposing Metropole Hotel on the corner of High Street and Jackson Street. In a previous incarnation it was called the New Bridge Inn. The Metropole Theatre was situated behind the hotel and opened in 1896, becoming the Scala Cinema in 1919. The theatre was demolished in 1960 though the original entrance to the cinema can be seen on the left of the building in the recent photograph.

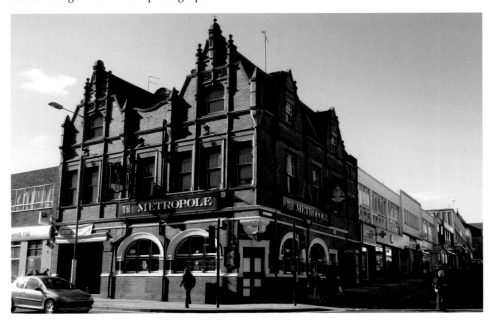

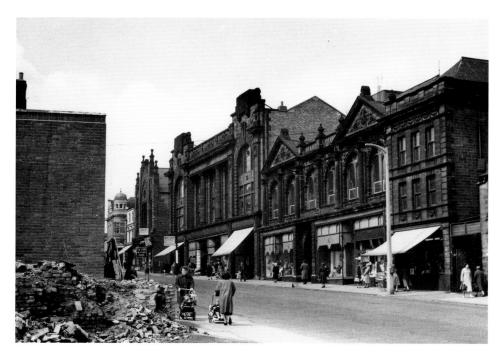

Remnants of Grandeur

Jackson Street in 1962. Jackson Street was known as 'Collier Chare' until the late seventeenth century, before then the area had been referred to as 'Jackson's Field' and then 'Jackson's Chare'. The Jackson in question is probably Henry Jackson, the estate steward to the Gerard family. The TSB bank is the second building from the top just up from the Co-op building and was built in 1881. It has been demolished, but the other distinctive buildings remain.

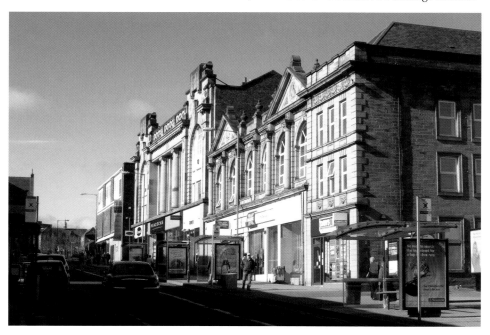

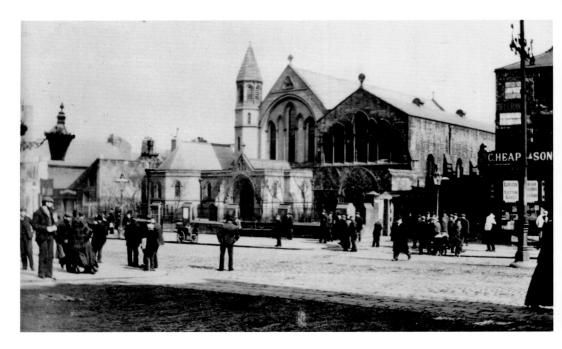

Medieval Remains

Holy Trinity Church on the High Street photographed around 1893. On this site was the Hospital of St. Edmund, founded in 1247 by Nicholas de Farnham, the Bishop of Durham. The oldest part of the building on the right is St. Edmund's Chapel, one of two medieval buildings in the town. After the reformation, the building fell into ruin and in 1836 the land was given by Cuthbert Ellison to the Rector of Gateshead. Public donations enabled the construction of Holy Trinity Church in 1837.

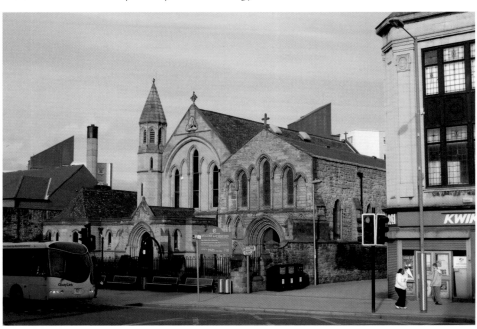

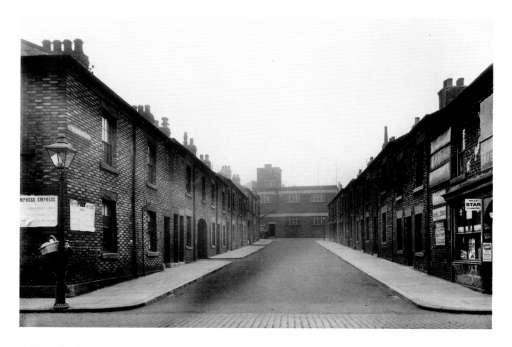

A Vanished Terrace

Clavering Street was built between 1851-1859 and was named after the famous Clavering family. James Clavering (1565-1630) was mayor of Newcastle, his grandson Sir James Clavering (1620-1702) served as High Sheriff of Durham, as MP for Durham and also as Mayor of Newcastle. Thomas Clavering established the family home at Axwell Hall in Blaydon in 1761. Clavering Street lay to the east of the High Street, connecting Trinity Street with Burdon Street. It was demolished in the 1930s and blocks of flats stand in its original position. The building in this recent photograph bears a strong resemblance to the one seen at the end of the street in the original.

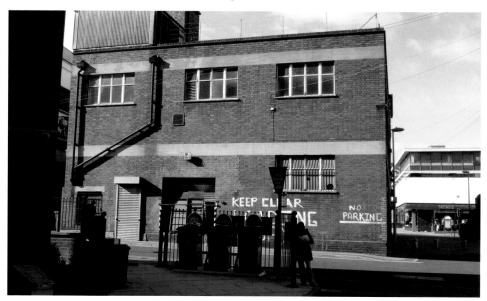

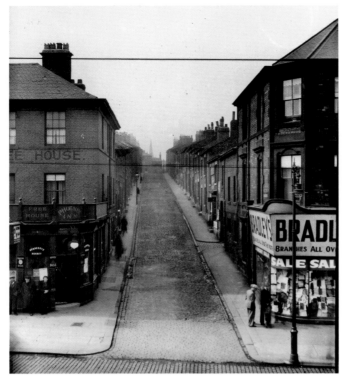

The Phoenix doesn't Rise Again!

The corner of the Phoenix Inn public house can be seen on the left hand side of this image taken in the 1930s. It was located at number 266 High Street on the corner of the High Street and Charles Street. The Phoenix is now called Curley's Bar and is currently up for lease. Charles Street was demolished in the 1940s so the angle of the street is different in the recent photograph.

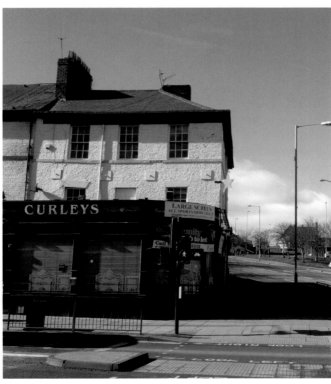

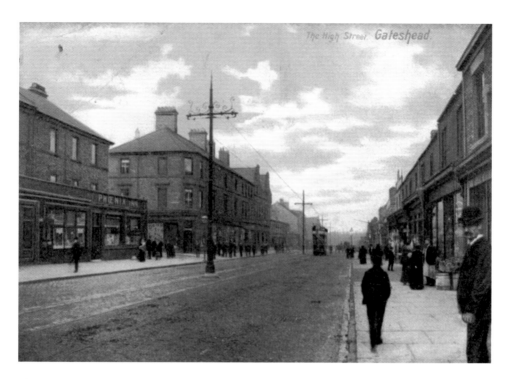

The Rise and Fall of the High Street

Another view of the Phoenix Inn on the High Street, looking north. The view is recognisable today only because of the presence of Curley's Bar on the corner.

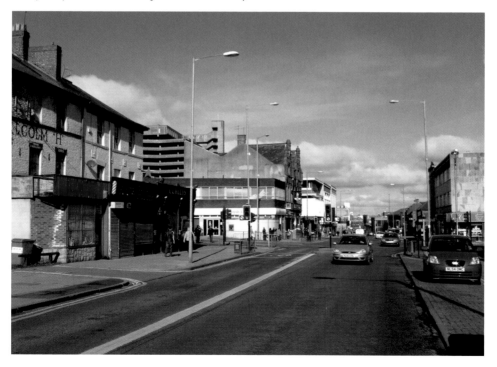

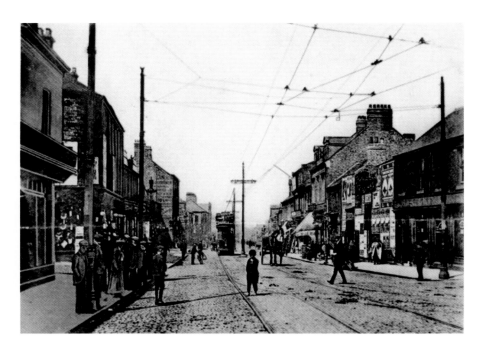

The 'dirty lane leading to Newcastle'

High Street looking north around 1900. The road on the left is Warwick Street. The Gateshead and District Tramways Company was formed in 1880, and Gateshead was unusual in that it never operated horse-drawn trams, perhaps because of the many steep hills. Instead the company utilised steam-powered and then electric trams. The conversion from steam to electric trams began in 1900 and the electric overhead wires can clearly be seen in this picture. By 1908 the Company was transporting over 10 million passengers per year. Only the street names allow these pictures to be compared, though the brick building on the central left looks the same.

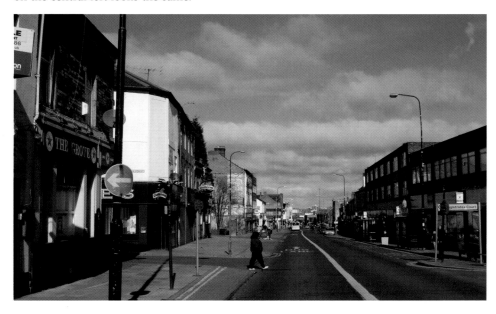

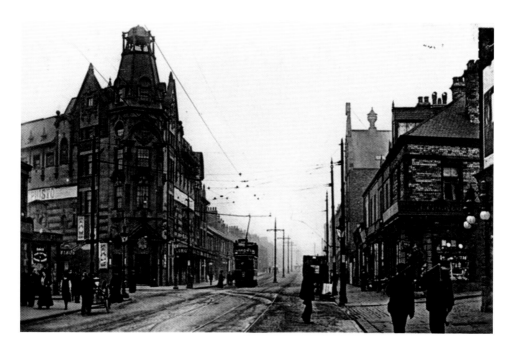

King's Theatre

This imposing building pictured around 1905. It stood on the corner of High Street and Sunderland Road; Warwick Street is on the right with Miss J. Turner's toyshop at 332 High Street (today it is the Grove pub). The theatre opened in 1905 with a presentation of the musical comedy 'Floradora'. It contained eighteen rows of seats, a promenade, and a saloon lounge over the main entrance and could hold around 2,000 people. It was renamed the Empire in 1918. In 1950 it became the Essoldo Cinema, closing in 1967 and demolished in 1968. The same view today; the street names enable comparison but the upper storey of the Grove appears to be original.

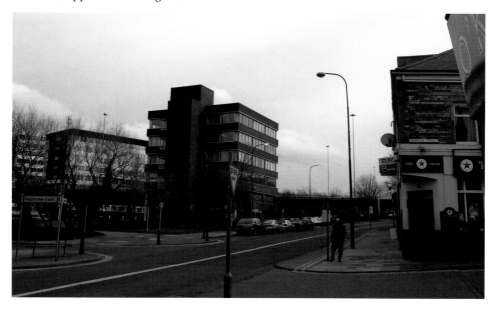

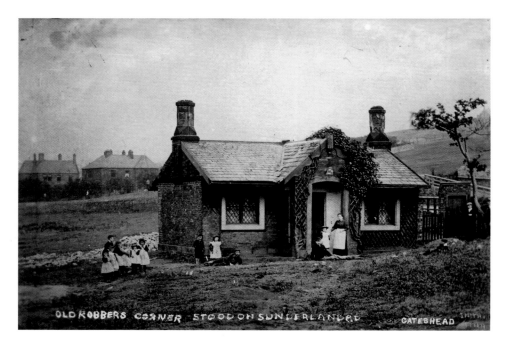

The Ginger Bread House

The cottage at 'Old Robber's Corner' was once the lodge of Park House and stood on Sunderland Road to the east of John Street. It is pictured around 1898 and there is some debate as to the name; one story suggesting that this was an isolated area frequented by highwaymen. Another possible explanation refers to the fact that 'robber' is a slang term used for the thistle plant, and this area was known to be covered with thistles. In the background, the house on the right is Ford House. This is the approximate location today, Ford House still exists as the convent to St Wilfrid's Catholic Church, but is hidden by the modern housing.

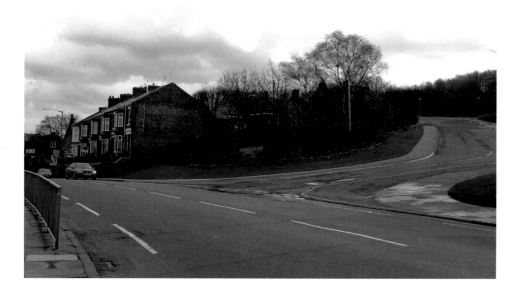

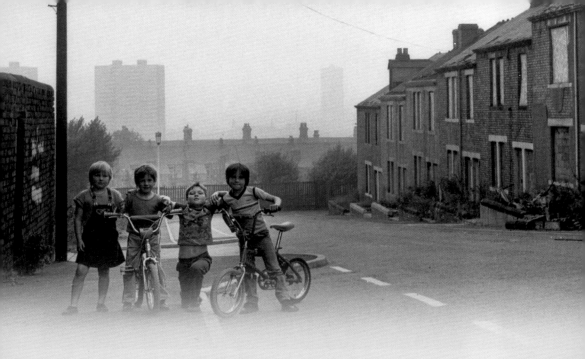

CHAPTER 3

Around Bensham

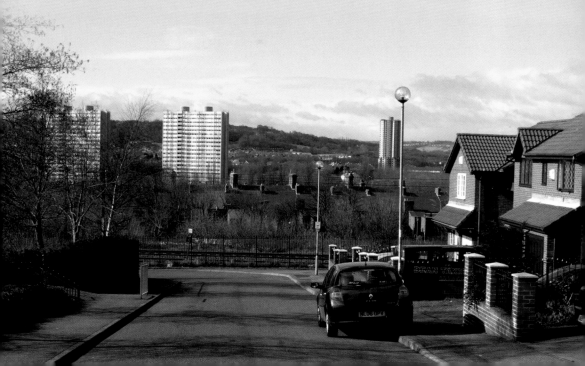

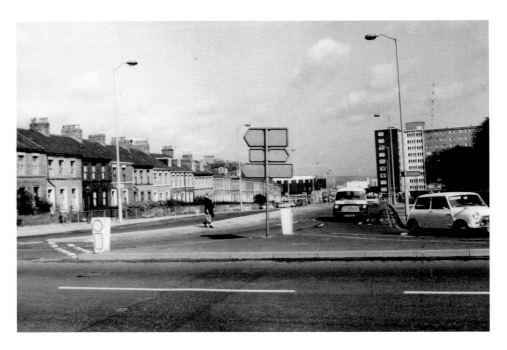

Regent Terrace

During the 1860s and 1870s the most sought after residences lay on Regent Terrace (built around 1852) Walker Terrace and Queens Terrace. Only wealthy industrialists such as coal owners, shipbrokers and their accountants could afford to live here. At that time these streets were surrounded by gardens and fields, Regent Terrace backed onto land belonging to the estate of the Shipcote family. The photograph above was taken in 1971 and this scene has barely changed, though the traffic is certainly busier.

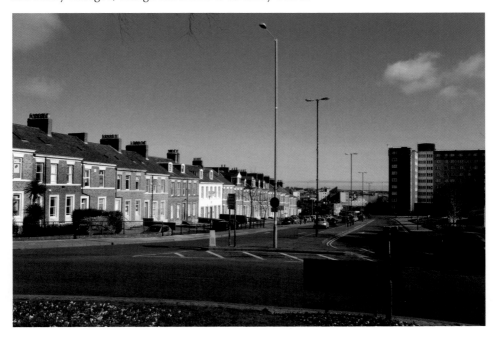

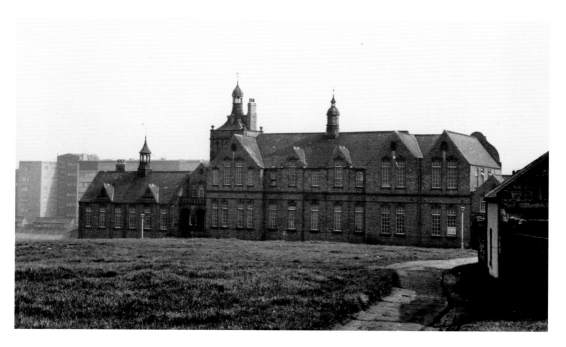

A Seat of Learning

This imposing building is Windmill Schools at Windmill Hills, off Bensham Road, pictured in 1964. It was originally the Day Industrial School for Boys and Girls and opened in 1880. It was designed by Thomas Oliver jnr. following architectural principles for school buildings outlined by E. R. Robson in 1874, himself a pupil of the famous architect John Dobson. Having spent so many years housing the youth of Gateshead it is somehow fitting that it ended its days as a care home for the elderly. I wonder if any the residents were themselves pupils in the same buildings many years ago?

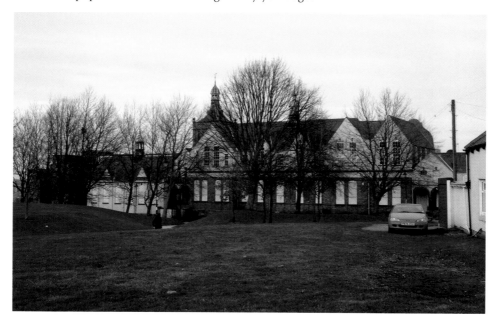

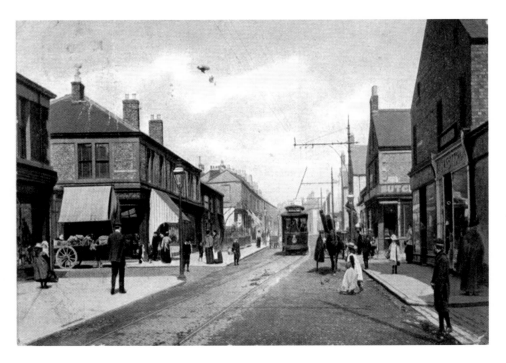

A Once Thriving Street

Coatsworth Road, *c.* 1910 looking north showing the junction with Claremont North and South Avenues on the right and Claremont Street on the left. This road was named after William Cotesworth, lord of the manor of Gateshead between 1716-1726, but note that when the road was named in 1892, it was misspelt! J. M. Shotton's confectioners on the right was at number 74, the corner of Eastman's butcher's shop can be seen further up on the right.

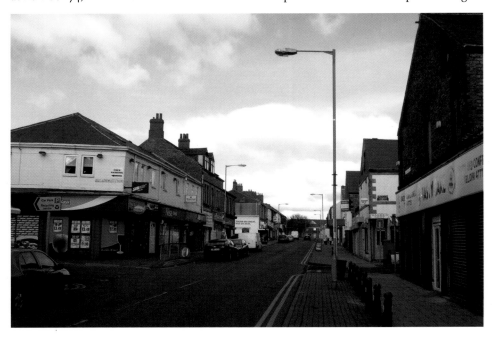

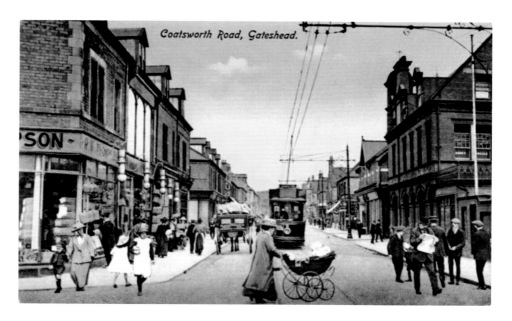

Coatsworth Road

Looking north, this is about 100 yards to the south of the location of the picture on the previous page. R. W. Thompson's ironmongers can be seen on the left and it stood at no. 137, across from the Honeysuckle Inn at no. 92. The overhead electric wires providing power to the tram can clearly be seen demonstrating that this scene was recorded after 1900. Some of the features of the original buildings can be seen in the recent picture.

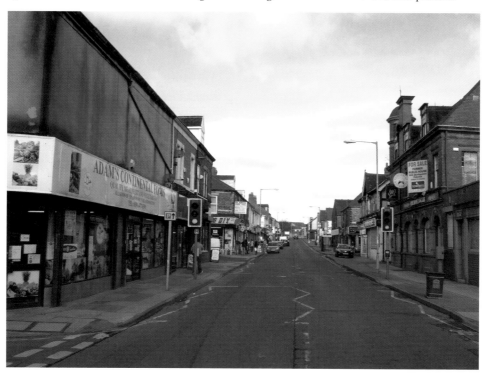

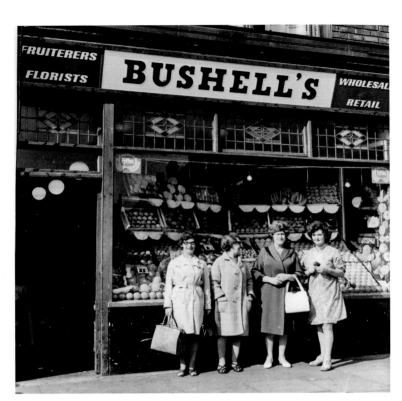

A Nation of Shopkeepers
Bushell's fruiterer's and florist's shop on Coatsworth Road, with some shoppers outside photographed in 1971. In Trade Directories, Bushell's is listed as having several premises around Gateshead. The exact location of this shop is unclear. Pictured below is Eric Briggs, owner of Station Stamp Shop with his son-in-law Steven Spoors and grandson Matthew Spoors.

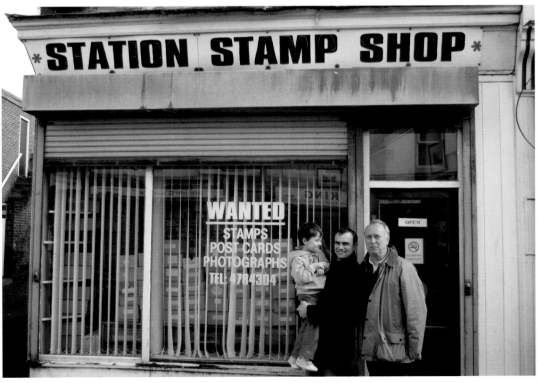

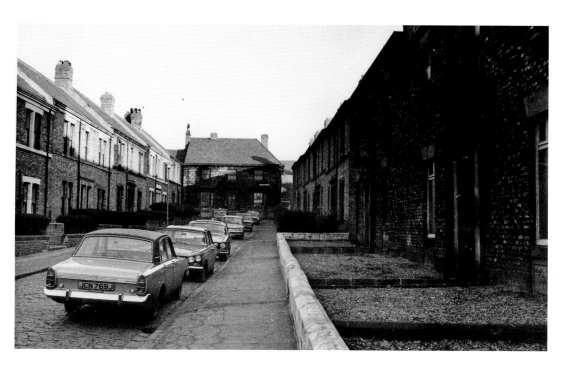

Villa Place

This lies off Coatsworth Road and is pictured around 1970. It is thought that this street is named after the imposing house that can be seen at the top. This is Woodbine Villa and would have been occupied by merchants and professionals, the surrounding terraced houses would have been for tradesmen. When the villa was first constructed it would have come with a large amount of land, a coach house and a stable for the horses.

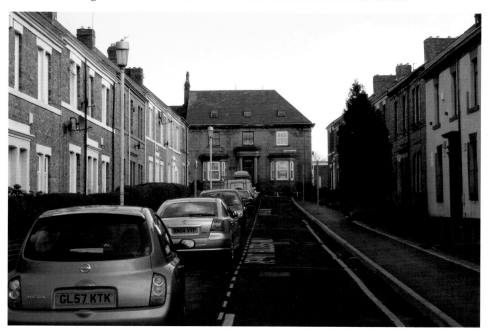

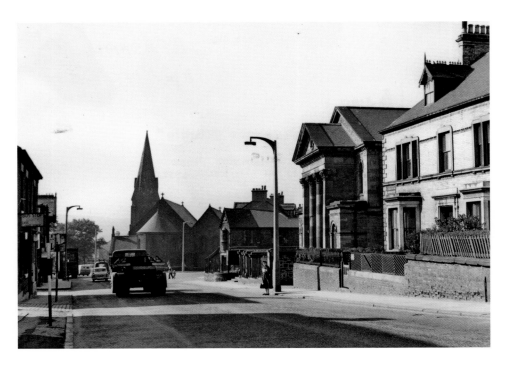

Bensham Road

Near the junction of Derwentwater Road and Cuthbert Street in 1960. St. Cuthbert's Church can be seen in the background. It was built between 1846-1848 to the designs of John Dobson, on land provided by the Askew family. The land around the church was prone to subsidence and the church was forced to close in the early 1990s. The imposing building on the right was a Methodist Chapel, now demolished.

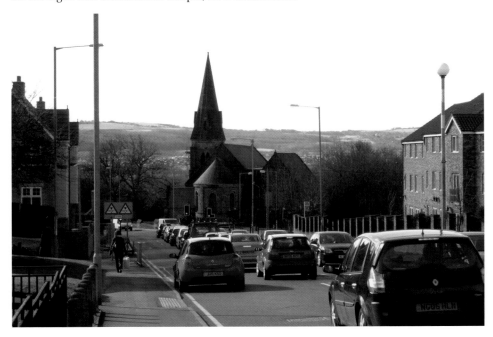

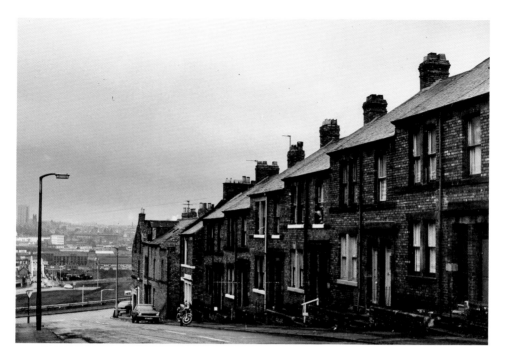

All Change!

Bank Street, Bensham. This row of terraced houses was demolished in the 1970s to make way for Saint Cuthbert's Village. Again, it is difficult to find the exact location, but the block of flats and the church in the far distance provide some reference point. The old Redheugh Bridge that can be seen to the left in the original picture was replaced by the new Redheugh Bridge in 1983.

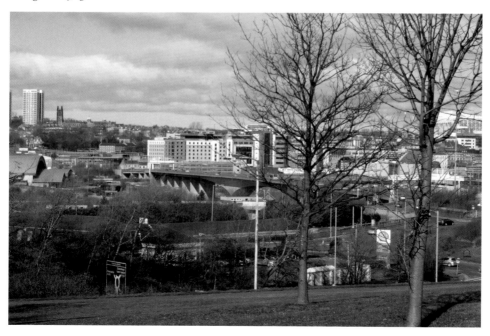

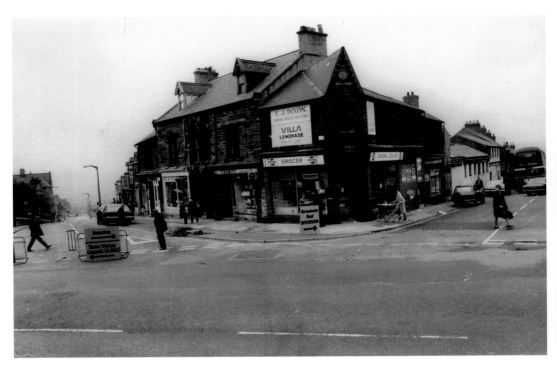

A Green Future?

The corner of Derwentwater Road and Cuthbert Street in 1972. All of this area has since been cleared to make way for new housing developments and access roads to the Redheugh Bridge.

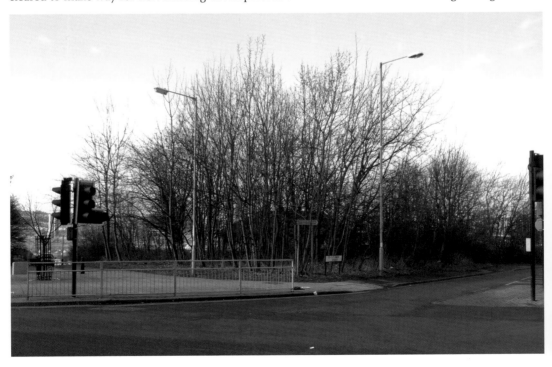

All Grown Up
St Cuthberts Street
in 1962. The street
remains but all of
the terraced housing
has gone, replaced
initially by the high–
rise development
St. Cuthbert's
Village, itself now
replaced by the
Windmill Hills
Estate and additional
green spaces
and recreational
facilities. The boy in
the picture would be
in his forties now.

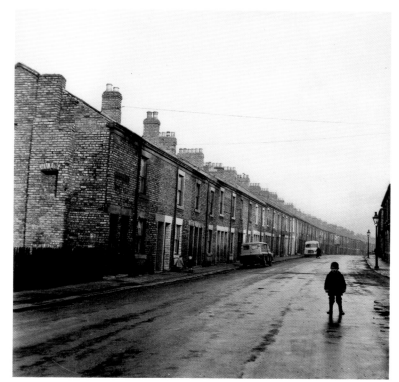

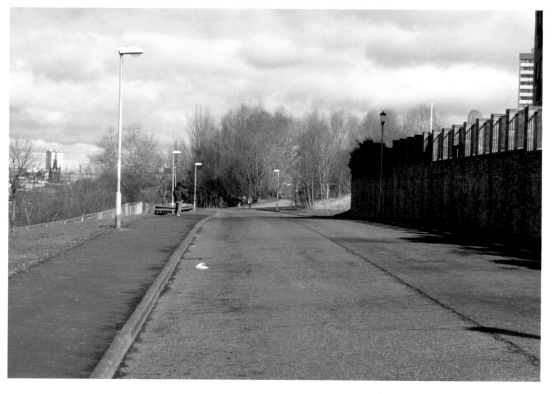

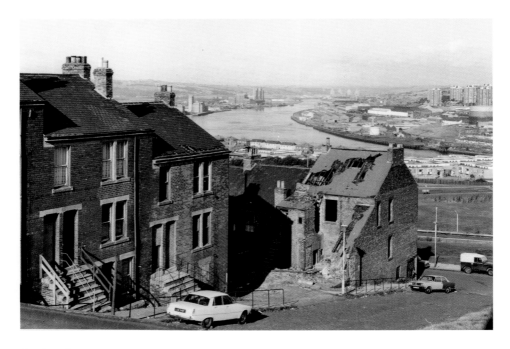

Gordon Street

Demolition during the 1970s. This area has been completely cleared and it is difficult to find its precise location. However the recent photograph is clearly in a similar location, with the curve of the river Tyne providing the backdrop. The new housing developments at Dunston can be seen on the left side of the river in the recent picture.

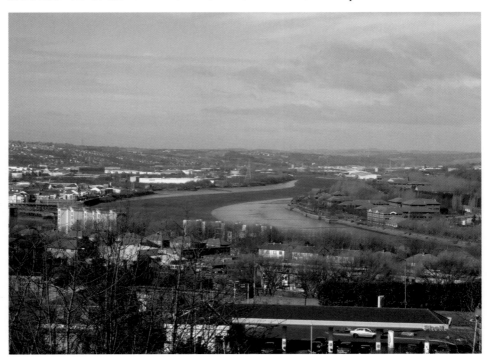

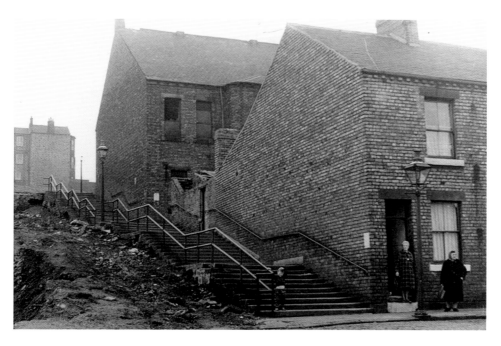

Stairway to Heaven?

Davison Street lying off St Cuthbert's Street/Bank Street demolished in 1970. The steep banks are still used to provide housing and the steps, though clearly new, are remarkably similar to the original ones, the new houses uncannily reflect the demolished properties.

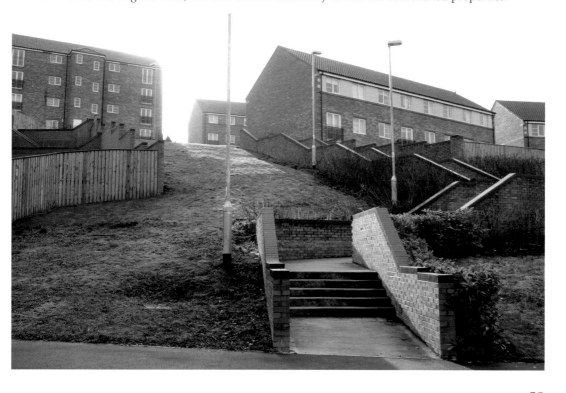

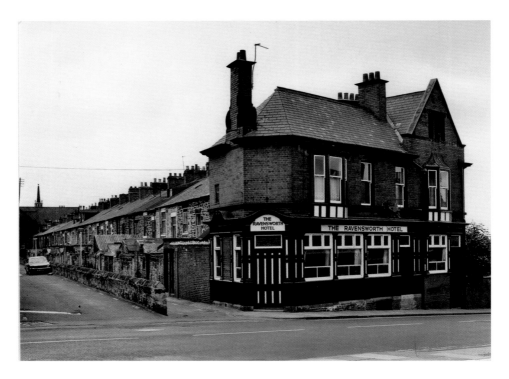

The Ravensworth Hotel

It is now called the Bensham Jockey. The row of houses on Ravensworth Terrace were demolished in 1985, and some of the houses were removed brick by brick and rebuilt at the town area in Beamish Museum, with the help of funding from various companies and local trusts.

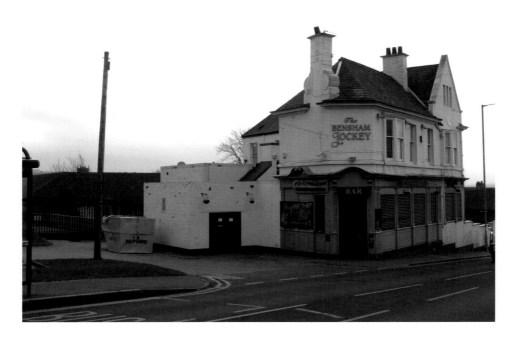

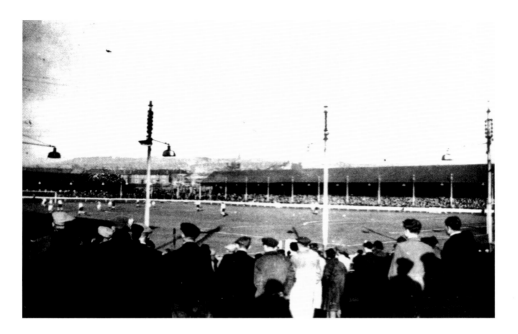

New Balls Please!

Gateshead FC were founded in 1930 and played at Redheugh Park, their highest home crowd being 20,752 against Lincoln City on 25 September 1937. This is the ground *c.* 1950 (floodlights were built in 1953), with the Askew Road stand in the background, the spire of St. Cuthbert's is just visible in the centre of the picture. The area still hosts football matches, Power League Group plc is home to eighty-four teams comprising eight adult and one junior leagues.

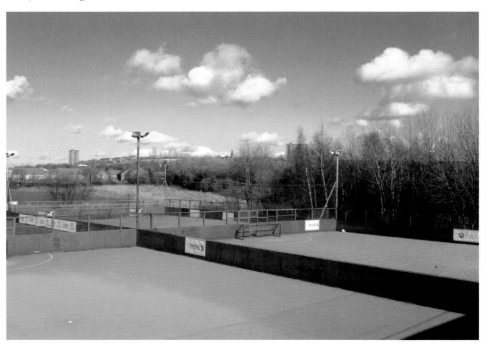

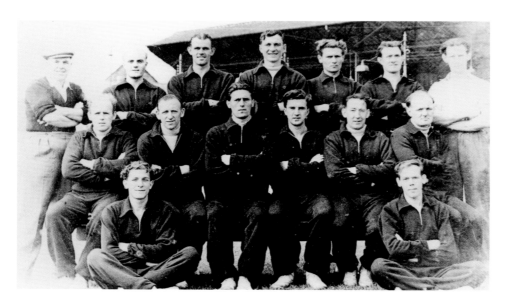

Gateshead FC

Pictured in the 1950s. Back Row from left- Bob Keen (Trainer), Fowler, Wyles, R. Gray, J. Callender, ??. Middle Row - L. Small, J. Woodburn, T. Callender, J. Campbell, W. Buchan, W. Cassidy. Front Row J. Ingham, J. Kendal.

The current squad for the 2009/2010 season are pictured below. Back Row (L to R). Carl Jones, Jamie Harwood, James Curtis, Paul Farman, Darren Forsythe, Stephane Pelonde, Craig Baxter. Middle Row (L to R). Graham Wood (Chairman), Wayne Phillips, Michael Mackay, Phil Turnbull, Chris Swailes, Jim Provett, Alex Francis, Graeme Armstrong, Neale McDermott, Steven Baptist, Brian Waites (Vice Chairman). Front Row (L to R). Martin Brittain, Phil Cave, Christoph Ascherl, Jeff Wrightson (Asst. Manager), Ian Bogie (Manager), Paul Thompson (Coach), Kris Gate, Mark Robinson, Steven Richardson.

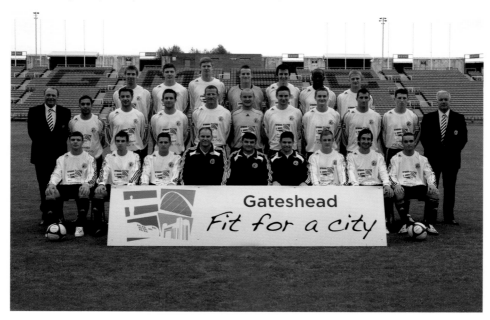

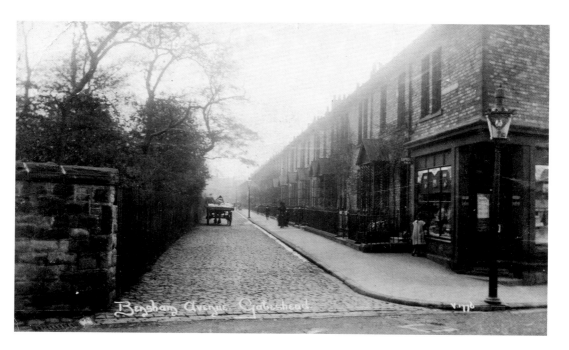

Bensham Avenue

The wall on the left is that of the former rectory that was formerly located near to St. Mary's. Further along the original wall is a blue plaque commemorating the rector's daughter Emily Davies (1830-1921) a pioneer for women's rights and female education. She was the founder of Girton College, Cambridge. The rectory was demolished in the 1960s.

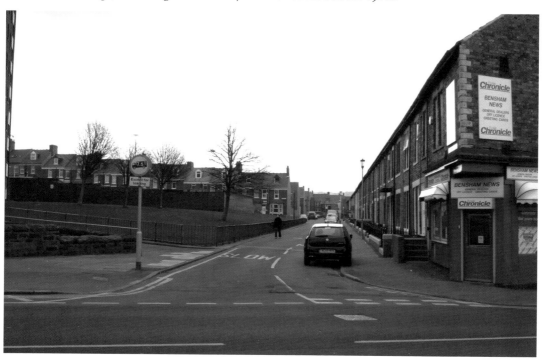

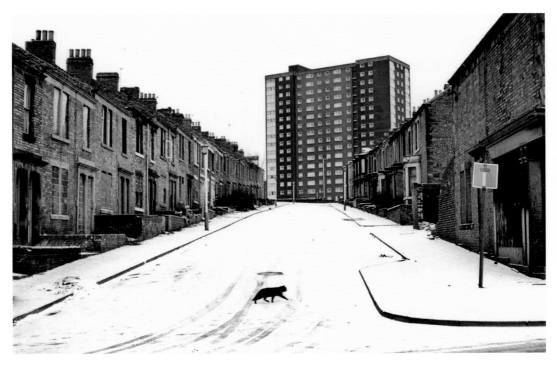

The Black Cat

Fourth Street in 1987. The terraced houses have gone but the block of flats provides a good reference point. Despite a long search I couldn't find any local pets to wander across the road!

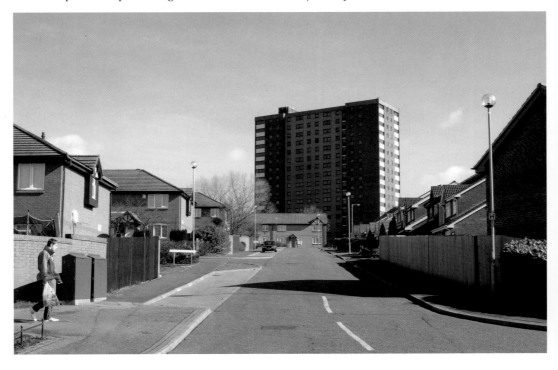

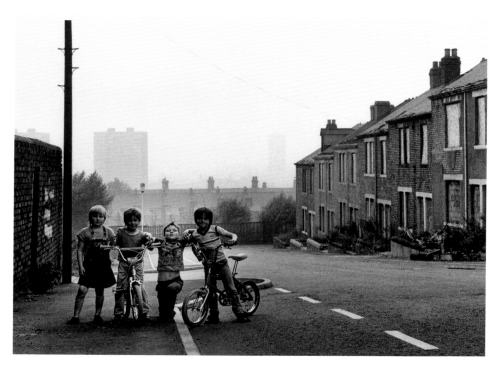

Four Pals

Alston Street looking down to the junction with Elysium Lane in 1985. The terrace on the right has been replaced by modern housing and the wall on the left has gone, but the block of flats and terrace in the distance can still be seen. In the background can be seen the Derwent Tower (called the 'Dunston Rocket') which was completed in 1971. The lads must be in their early thirties now – I wonder who they are?

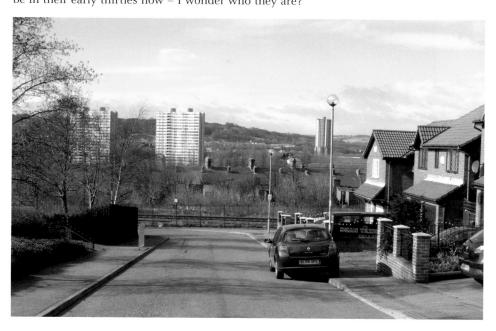

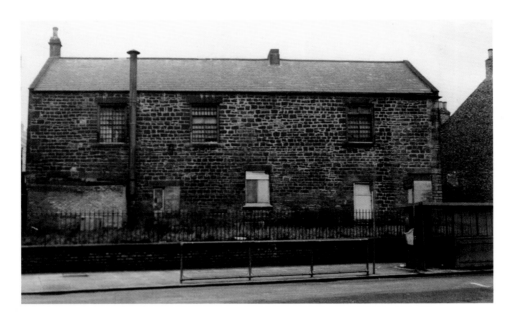

Bensham Asylum

This was built around 1799 on Sidney Grove, the above photograph being taken in 1971. Before being demolished in the 1970s the asylum was a launderette. This house is in the approximate location of the asylum and when it was being built in 1989 the cellars to the asylum caused problems for the foundations of the garage. The house is currently owned by Kevin Watkins who was surprised to hear of the former property where his house now stands.

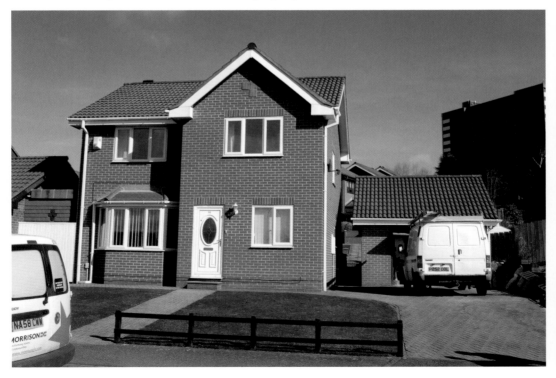

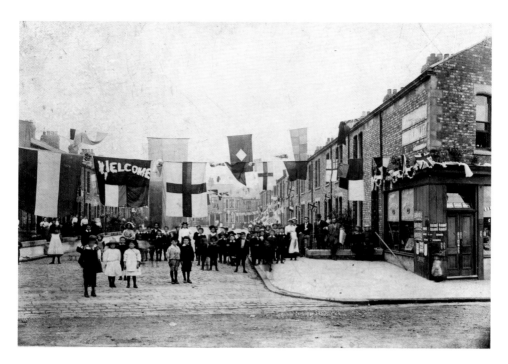

A Mystery Celebration

Newton Street, Bensham in 1902. There is clearly a celebration being held but there is some debate as to what is being celebrated. One theory suggests that the celebration is for the coronation of Edward VII that took place in 1902, though a banner clearly says 'welcome' so another suggestion is that they are celebrating the return of local soldiers from the Boer War which ended in the same year.

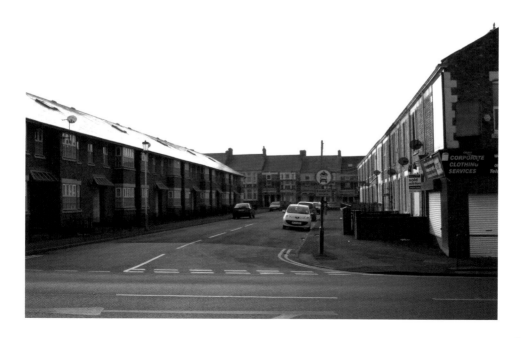

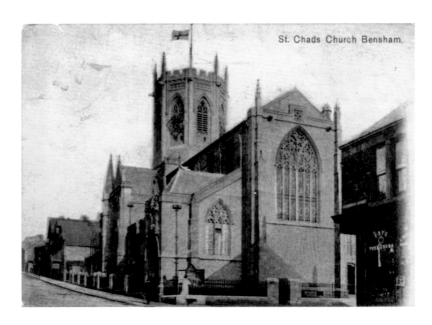

St. Chads Church Bensham.

St. Chad's Church

This imposing building sits on the corner of Rawling Road and Westminster Street. Lord Northbourne donated land for the construction of this church in 1895 but the final impressive result was not possible without the financial patronage of Emily Easton. The church was designed by local architect W. S. Hicks and was completed in 1903. The stained glass window in the western side is a tribute to the architect who died before his creation was completed, while the north transept window commemorates its patron, Emily Easton. It is a striking building with the octagonal tower being its distinctive feature, and it fortunately remains untouched by time.

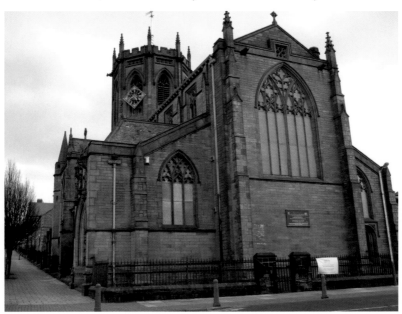

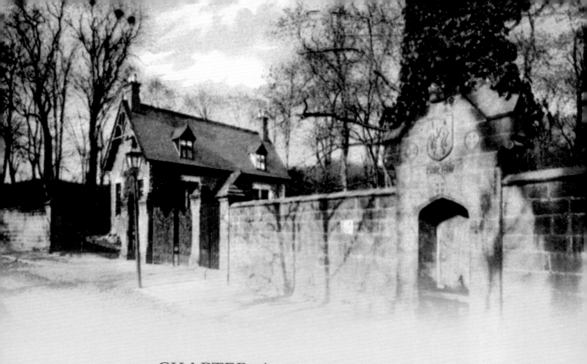

CHAPTER 4

Around Saltwell Road

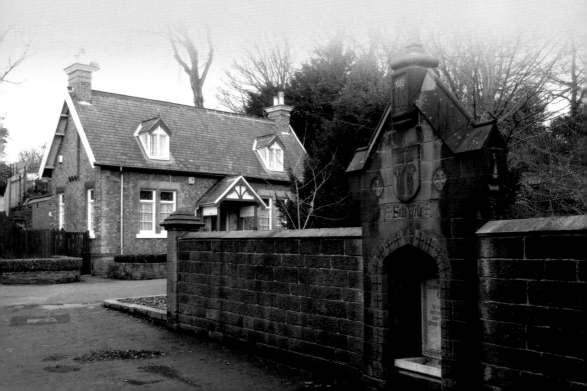

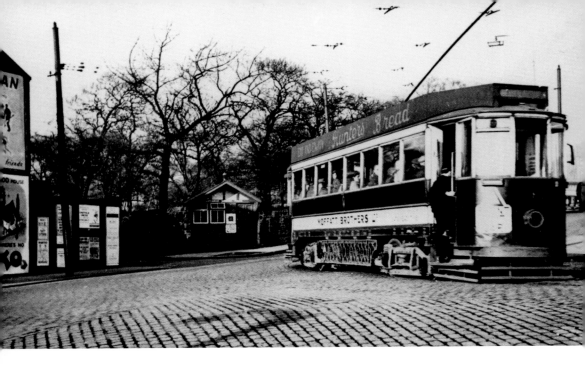

Cobbled Memories

Bensham Bank, with a tram turning into Saltwell Road. The Gateshead and District Tramways Company built three routes, one to Heworth, one to Teams, and one to Low Fell and extensions were constructed to Dunston and Ravensworth Waggonway in 1903, additional extensions were created in 1909 to Saltwell Cemetery and Springwell Road.

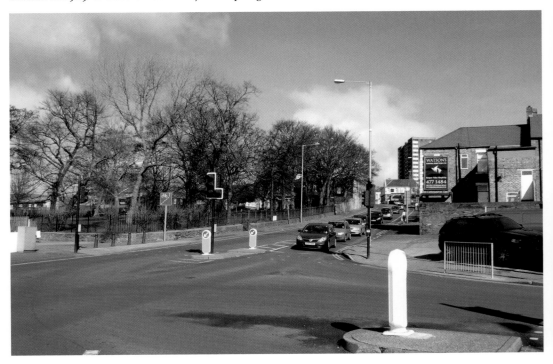

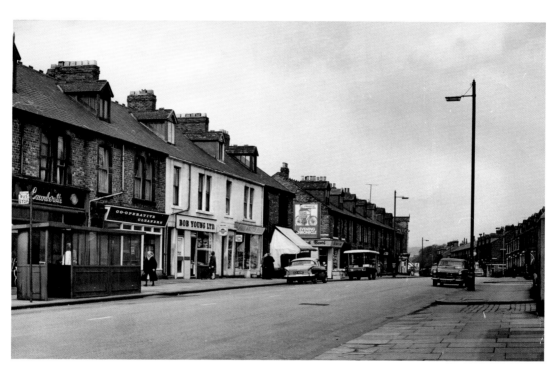

Saltwell Road
Pictured in the 1960s. The shops have clearly altered, but the pictures can be matched by looking at the gabled windows and the distinctive chimneys on the row of houses on the left hand side.

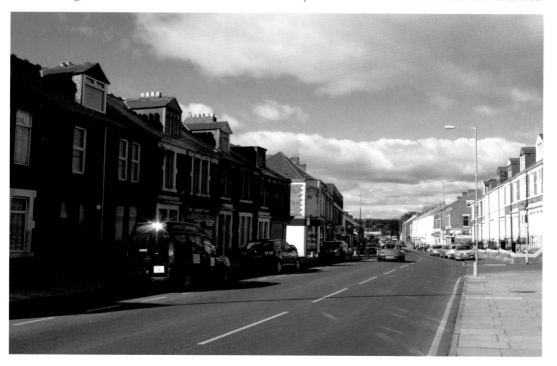

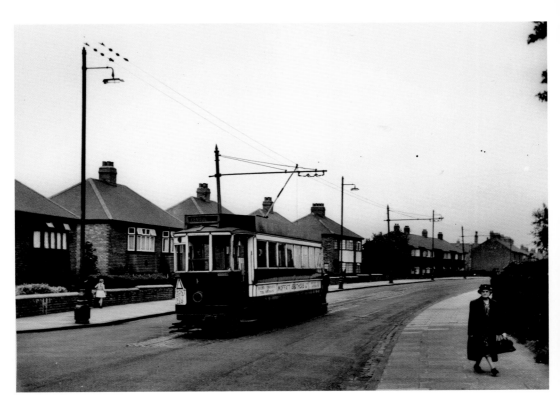

Any More Fares?
A tram on Saltwell Road in 1950. The houses on the left have barely changed in fifty years, though their windows have been updated and their hedges have grown!

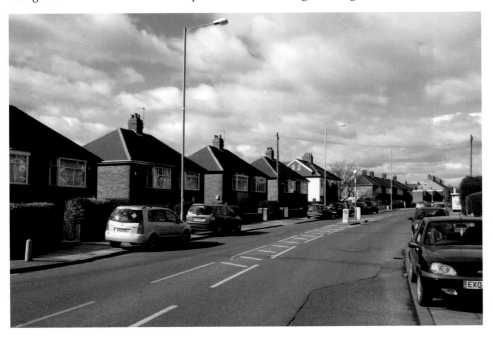

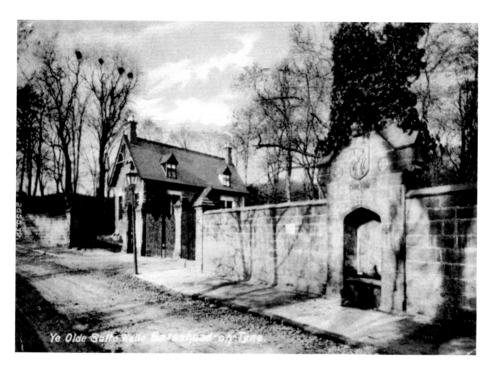

Drink Up

Before the days of piped water, the citizens of Gateshead would have to use wells dotted around their town. The wells were named after their locations or by the taste or quality of their water. This is the Salte Well constructed in 1872, from which we derive 'Saltwell' and presumably had a salty taste. It was renowned for its healing properties.

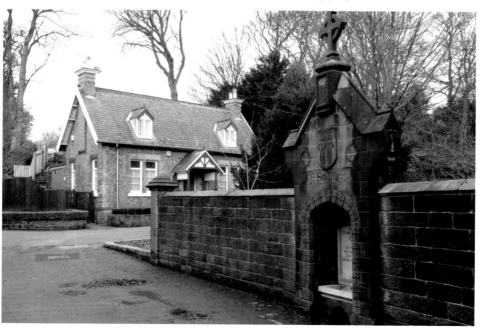

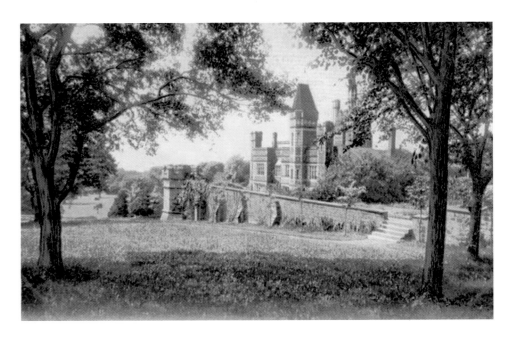

The Towers Reborn

Saltwell Park was created for public use in 1876 on the estate owned by stained glass manufacturer William Wailes. An agreement was reached with the Council and around 60 acres of land was purchased for £35,000, this included Saltwell Towers but the Wailes family were allowed to remain in their home as tenants, paying £140 per year. The park was designed by Edward Kemp, who had assisted Joseph Paxton in creating the famous park at Birkenhead. The maze opened in 1877 and the lake was added in 1880. Over the years the park became dilapidated, but a £10 million grant from the Heritage Lottery Fund in 1999 enabled the grounds to be restored to their former Victorian glory. The park re-opened fully in 2004 and Saltwell Towers was also renovated, and is now a popular Visitor Centre and café.

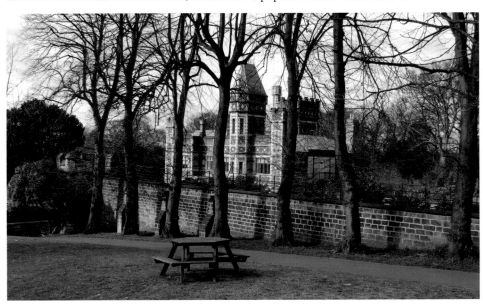

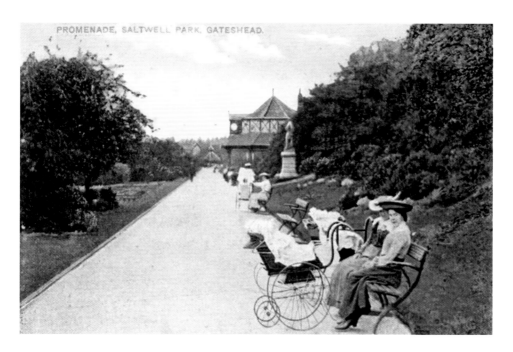

A Sunday Promenade

This is the promenade, also known as the Broad Walk, and was the first section of the park to be designed by Edward Kemp. The Broad Walk was separated from the fields at the northern end by a large hedge which was not just decorative. The fields could be rented out for livestock and the hedge prevented them straying into the park and consuming the carefully laid out gardens and shrubs! The statue on the right is Alderman John Lucas (1837-1900) and was installed in 1903.

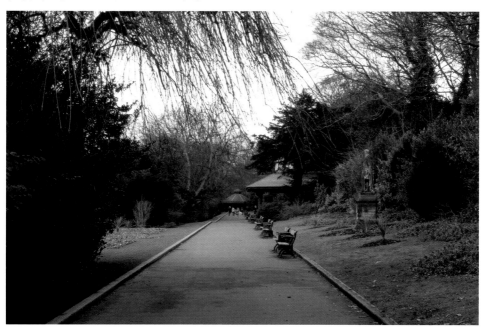

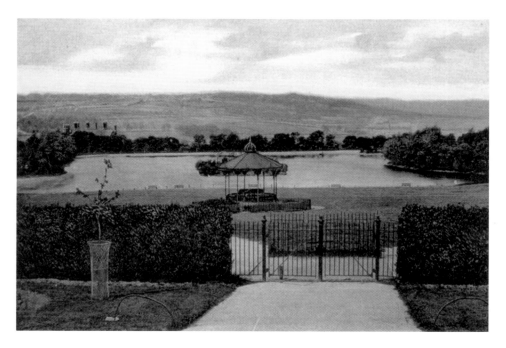

Still a Scenic View

The view looking over the lake with Team Valley and Lobley Hill in the distance. The bandstand was moved to several different locations around the park with some photographs showing it housed on the island in the middle of the lake. The original structure was moved to Beamish Museum in 1975 and formed the first development in the town area.

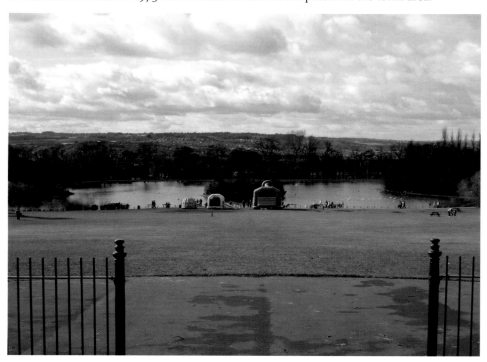

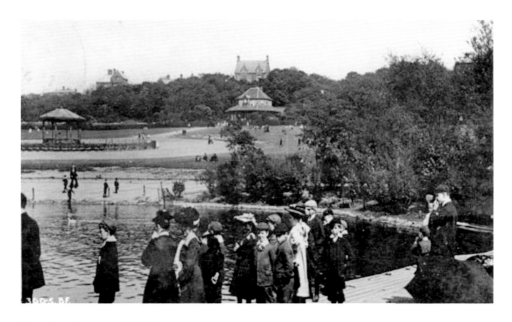

Messing about on the Water

A stroll around the gardens, dene and especially the lake has been a weekend activity for the families of Gateshead since the park opened. The more adventurous can hire a rowing boat and chase the over-fed ducks and geese.

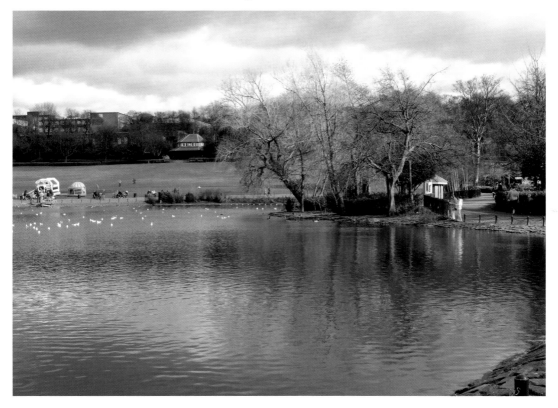

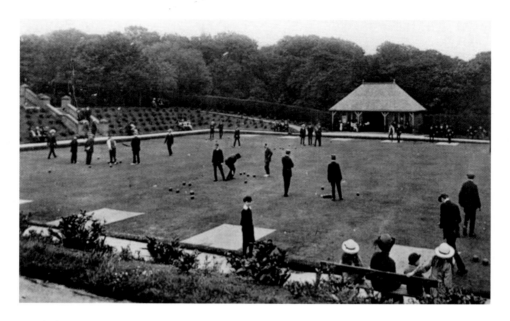

Bowled Over!

A genteel game of bowls in Saltwell Park around the turn of the 1900s. This remains a popular pastime in the park, and the bowls club can often be seen practicing, and playing their matches. The original steps are still present on the left, but the pavilion has changed.

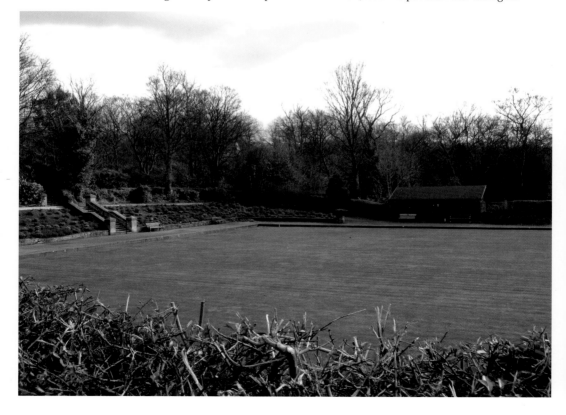

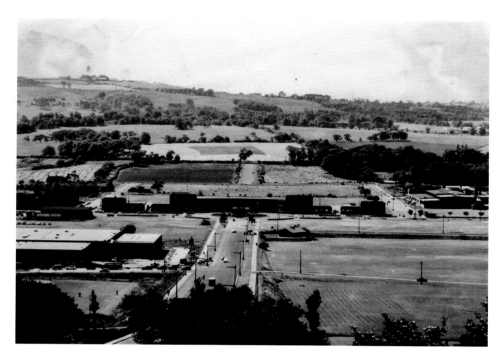

Team Valley Trading Estate

Looking west along Eastern Avenue, *c.* 1961. On its construction the central road Kingsway was one of the widest in the country, the planners also factored in additional services, leisure facilities and plenty of open spaces with tree-lined avenues. The site continues to evolve and contains the highest concentration of employment opportunities in Gateshead. The building in the centre of the old image is St George's House and can barely be seen in the new photograph.

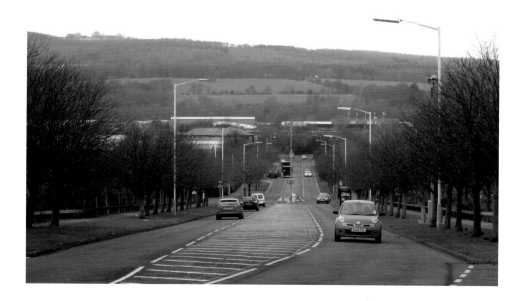

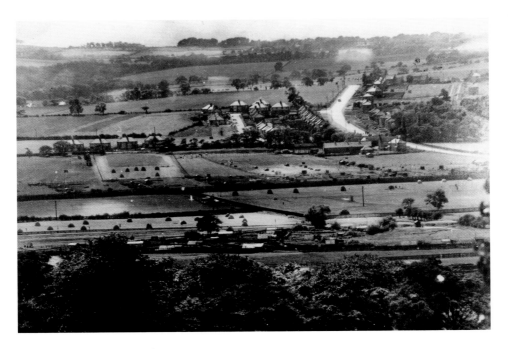

What Happened to the View?

Team Valley circa 1934 before the construction of Team Valley Trading Estate. Lobley Hill can be seen in the background, the hay stooks belong to Norwood farm. The Estate was planned during the inter-war years as a means of relieving unemployment by creating a large site for smaller industries. Construction began in 1936 and the 700 acre site was opened by King George VI on 22 February 1939. The clump of trees on the brow of the hill provides a useful comparison point.

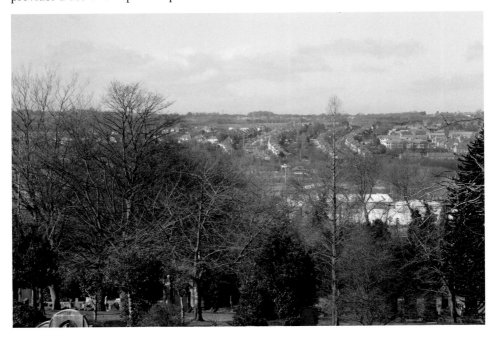

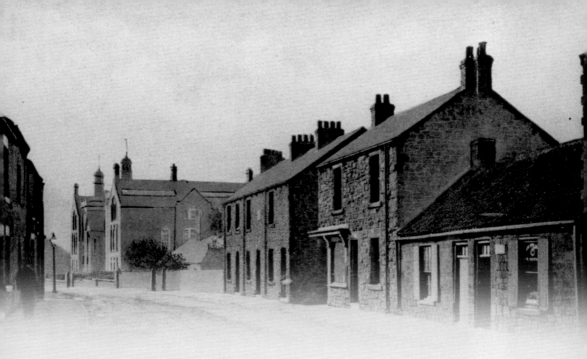

CHAPTER 5

Low Fell and Beyond

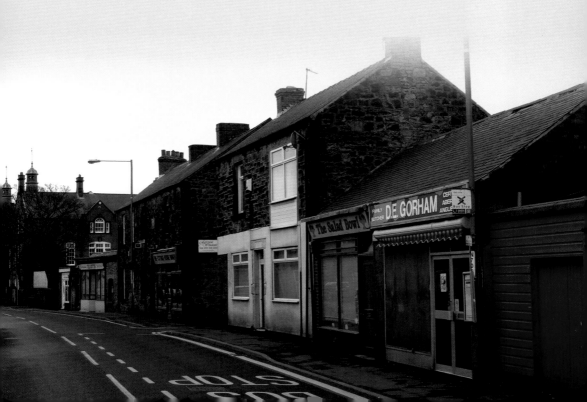

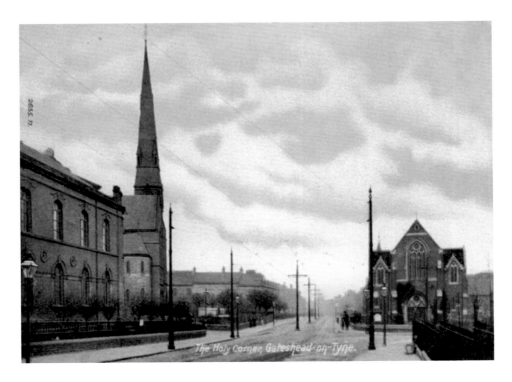

Amen Corner

The junction of High Street West, Durham Road and Gladstone Terrace. The three churches, the Baptist Chapel (first building on the left), the Presbyterian Church (with the spire) and the United Free Methodist Church (on the right) led to the name 'Holy Corner' and 'Amen Corner'. Much of this area was demolished during the 1950s to make way for Gateshead Highway, but the Baptist Chapel survives as Durham Road Baptist Church.

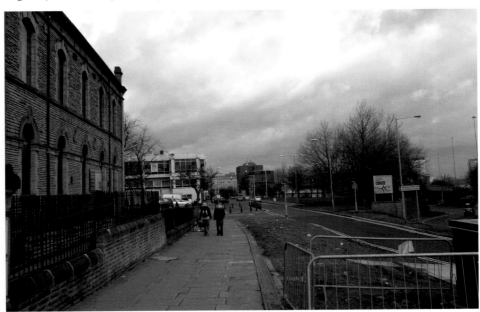

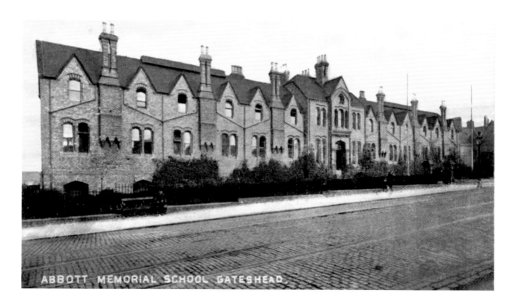

Gone but Hopefully not Forgotten

The Abbot School just down from Amen Corner was built in 1869 and was the first building on Durham Road. It was established to provide an education to 'street children', the money being provided by the widow of noted industrialist John Abbot. The school closed in 1930 and was demolished in 1968.

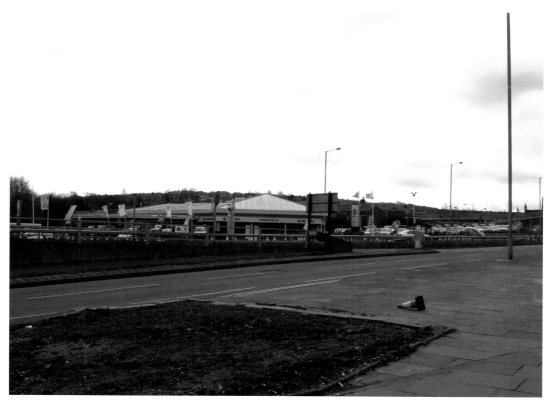

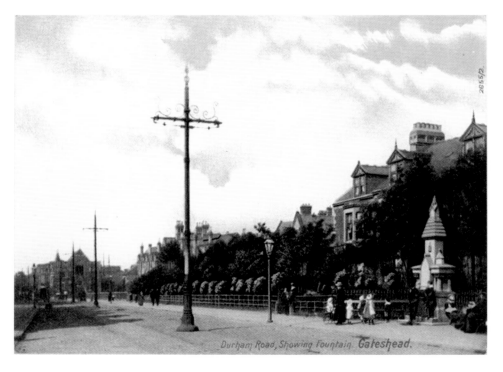

A Quiet and Peaceful Street (once)

A genteel Durham Road with the drinking fountain sited opposite Whitehall Road, and just short of St. Edmund's Road (out of shot). In the distance can be seen 'Holy Corner', with the Methodist Church being clearly visible. The recent view could hardly be more different!

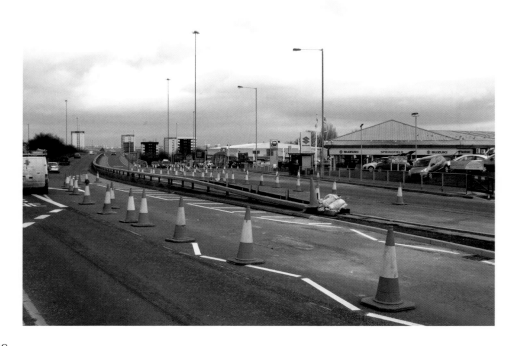

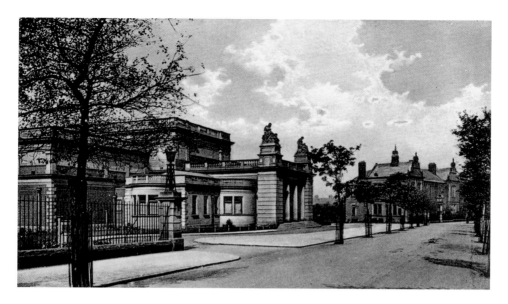

A House of Art

The Shipley Art Gallery is named after Joseph Shipley, a wealthy solicitor who bequeathed the sum of £30,000 for the construction of a gallery to house his art collection somewhere in Newcastle. His generous offer was refused, and so he turned to Gateshead who gladly accepted, and it was constructed on Prince Consort Road in 1915. The designer Arthur Stockwell also planned the adjacent Gateshead Public Library but complications in obtaining the funding meant that a scaled-down version wasn't completed until 1926, after his death.

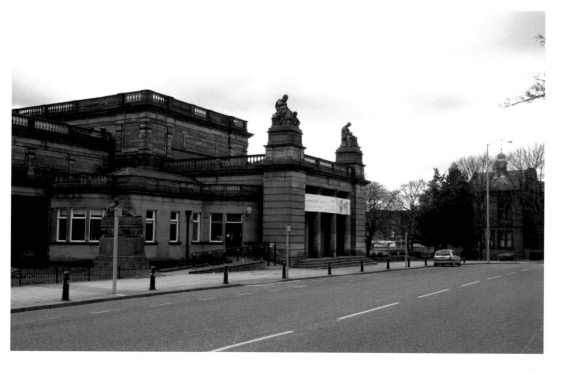

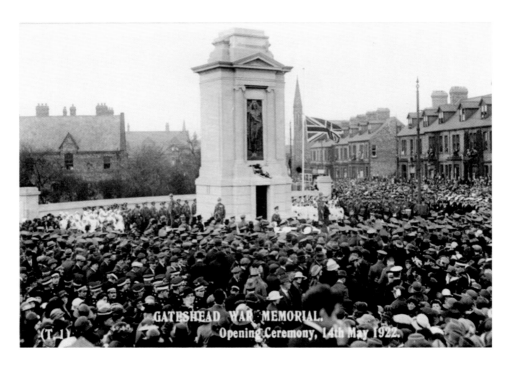

GATESHEAD WAR MEMORIAL.
(T.1) Opening Ceremony, 14th May 1922.

Lest We Forget...

The opening ceremony of the Gateshead War Memorial on 14 May, 1922 at the corner of Prince Consort Road and Durham Road. The Lord Bishop of Durham is in the act of dedicating the Memorial that would then serve as a poignant reminder to future generations as the immense losses during the First World War, and in subsequent conflicts. The spire of St. Marks is more clearly seen in the original picture.

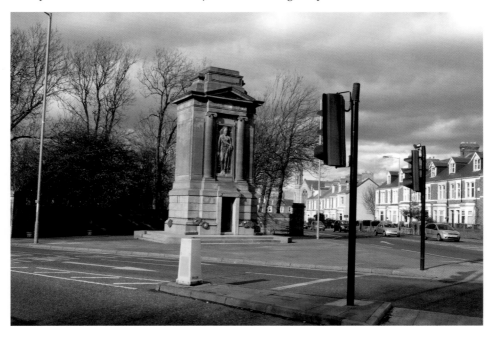

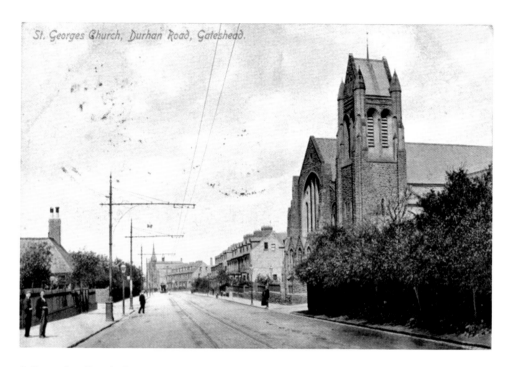

St. Georges Church, Durham Road, Gateshead.

A Towering Reminder

St George's Church, Durham Road before 1906. This church was built between 1894-1897 to the designs of Stephen Piper, a local architect. Much of the furniture is original and the organ built in 1901 by Henry Willis is felt to be a particularly fine example of his work. The current view of this fabulous building is somewhat ruined by the footbridge! The spire of St. Mark's (built in 1906) can just be seen in the recent picture.

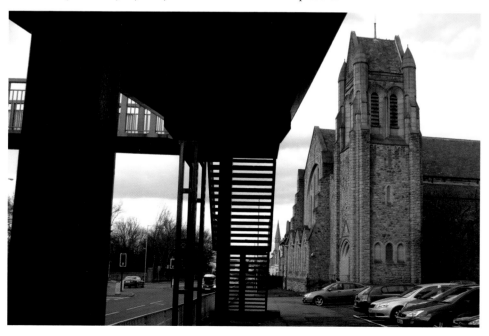

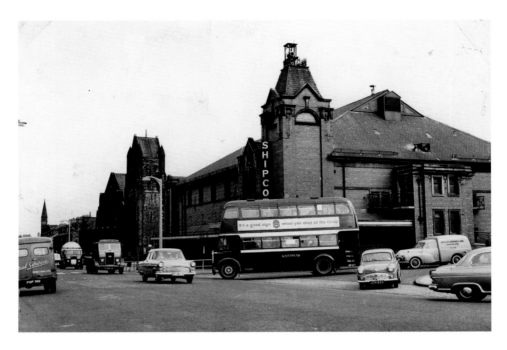

Pot Black!

Shipcote Picture Hall at the junction of Dryden Road and Durham Road, around 1960. The Picture Hall opened in 1911 and was famous for the very high standard of its resident orchestra. The hall was extended during the 1930s, and over 1,200 people squeezed themselves inside to watch films such as *Follow the Fleet* which was the most popular film to show at the Hall in its history. It closed in 1960 with the film *Journey to the Centre of the Earth* being its final screening. To the immediate left of the Picture Hall is St. George's Church, on the far left is St. Mark's Church. It is now a Snooker Hall.

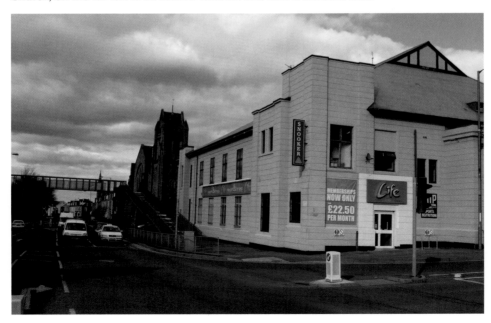

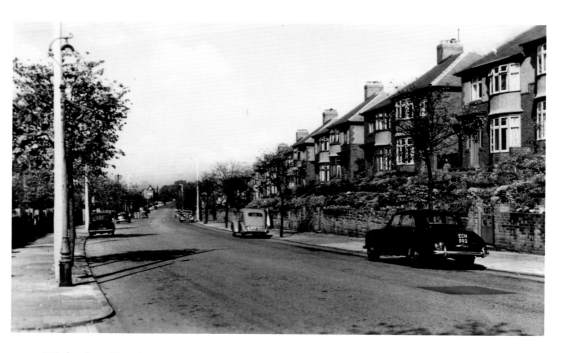

A Suburban Street

This is Dryden Road, named after Dryden's farm which stood on the site of the current fire station. A rough farm track led between the fields right up to Kells Lane, this track being called Dryden Lane. In the late 1930s Low Fell had become a very desirable place to live and many private houses were built in the surrounding fields. Dryden's farm and others nearby had disappeared by the Second World War and the sprawl of houses further expanded. Little has changed but the trees have certainly flourished.

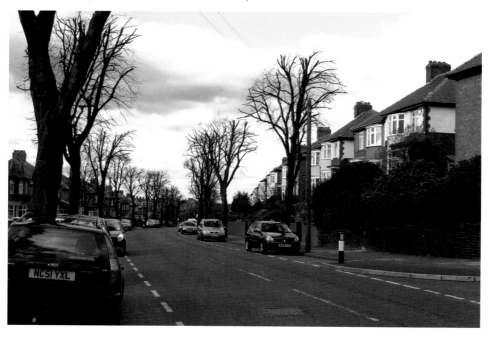

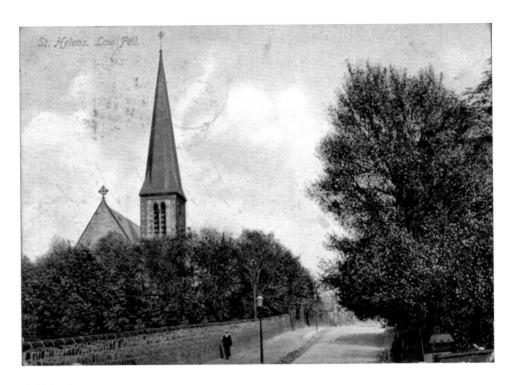

St Helen's

The church sits on on Belle Vue bank and was constructed in 1876. At the time this was taken around 1900, the Bank was clearly a leafy side road branching off from Durham Road. The road is no longer a leafy side street but a busy route between Saltwell Road and Durham Road.

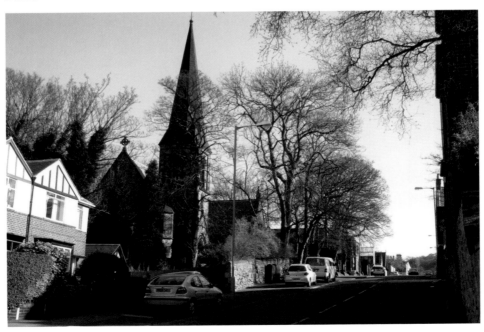

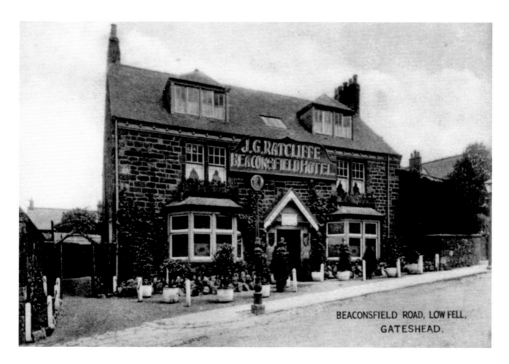

BEACONSFIELD ROAD, LOW FELL,
GATESHEAD.

The Comfort of the Familiar

The Beaconsfield Hotel on Beaconsfield Road. The road led to Beaconsfield House but was originally called Buck Lane, after the public house The Buck on its north side. Buck Lane became Beaconsfield Road in 1895. The pub is now called The Beaconsfield.

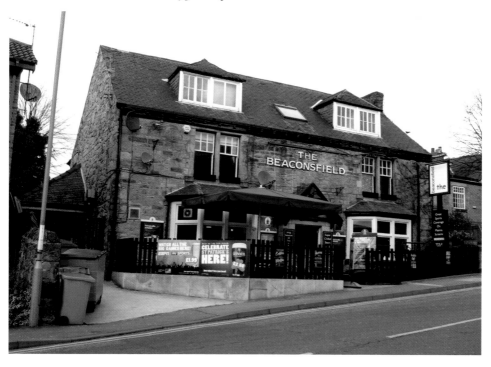

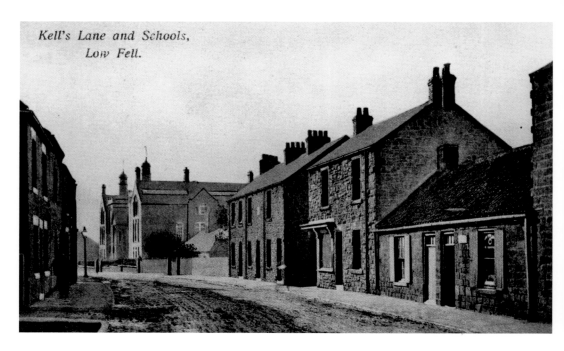

Kell's Lane and Schools, Low Fell.

Kells Lane

It is often assumed that Kells Lane was named in honour of William Kell, Gateshead's first Town Clerk, but it is possible that it refers to Richard Kell the quarry owner of Windy Nook. Indeed the name Kell had been used on maps predating William Kell. The large building at the curve in the road is the school.

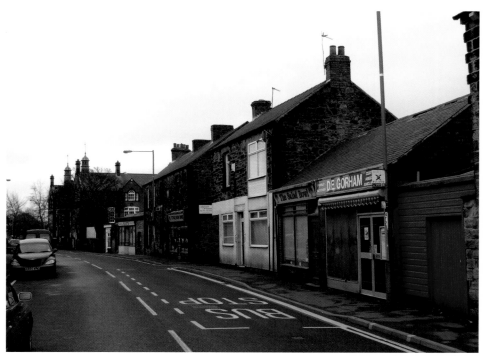

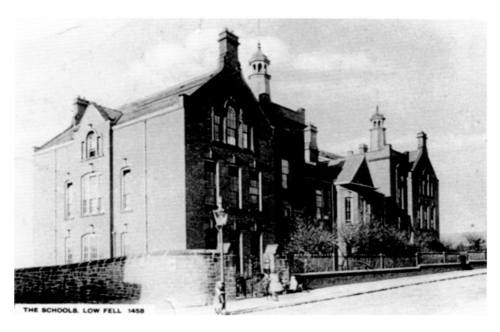

THE SCHOOLS, LOW FELL 1458

The School

This started life as Low Fell Board School and is now Kells Lane County Primary School, the trees have certainly thrived and the external appearance of the building has changed little.

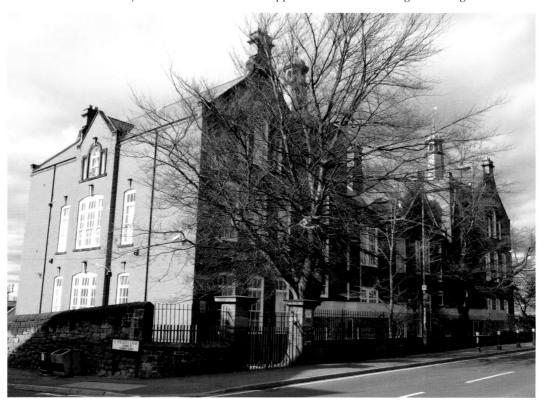

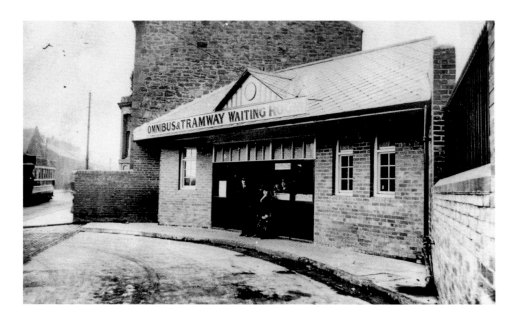

A Long Wait?

The omnibus and tramway waiting room at the junction of Durham Road and Kells Lane. The Gateshead and District Tramway Company had obtained the right to operate motorised buses alongside its trams in 1909 and so this picture must have been taken after that date. The motor buses were very popular because of their speed and the fact that they could overtake the more lumbering trams running along their fixed rails. They also enabled smaller towns and villages to be connected to the larger towns and urban centres and thus for the first time could easily commute to find work further afield. Currently it is a locksmith's, but is easily recognisable.

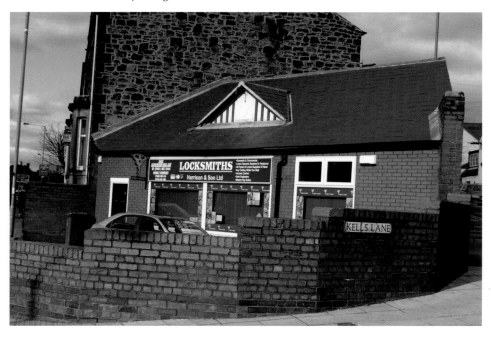

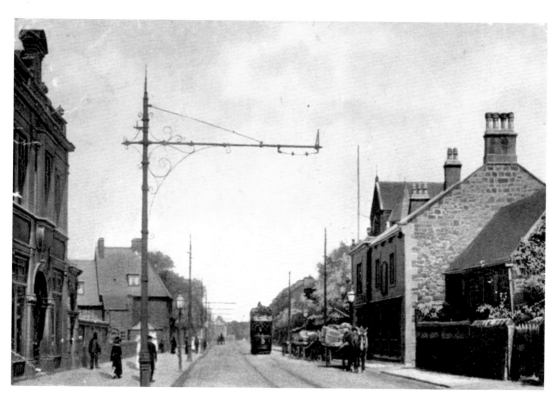

Horse, Tram and Car

Durham Road looking North. The upper storey of the building on the left remains as it was. The building on the right is also mostly unchanged, it is the Southern Memorial and is now adjacent to the Wesley Memorial Methodist Church and the Gateshead Arms.

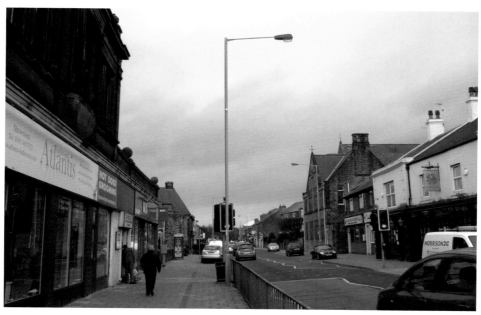

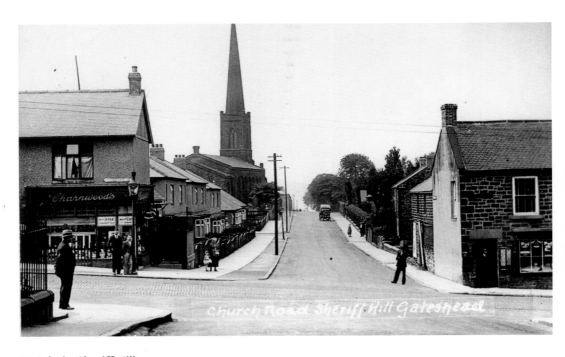

St. John's, Sheriff Hill

The church of St. John the Evangelist on Church Road. It was constructed in 1824-5 to designs by John Ions. The church is a modest building but the spire can be seen for miles around. It has a large churchyard containing a tall obelisk that commemorates a quarry owner killed in a railway accident in 1840.

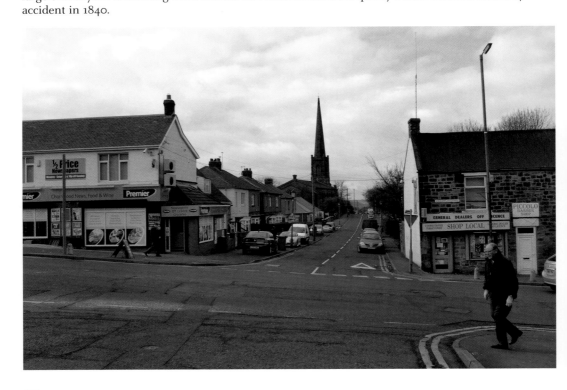

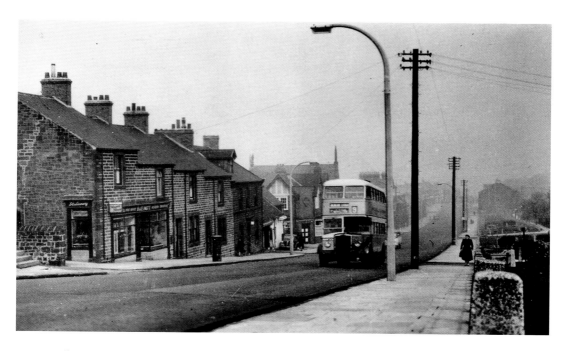

Sodhouse Bank

Sheriff's Highway, Sheriff Hill, photographed in the 1950s. The road was originally called Sodhouse Bank after the many huts constructed by tinkers out of turf or sod that lined the street. Sheriff Hill is so named because in the thirteenth century it was the meeting place of judges of assize and the sheriffs of Newcastle. The mock-tudor fronted building is the Three Tuns.

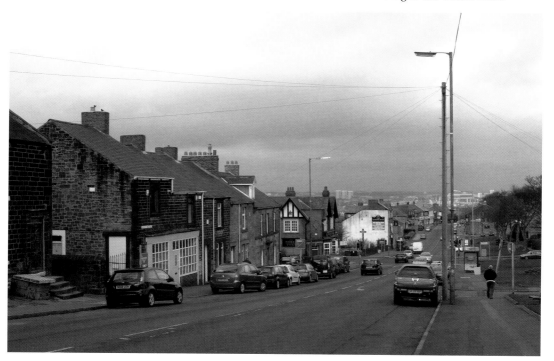

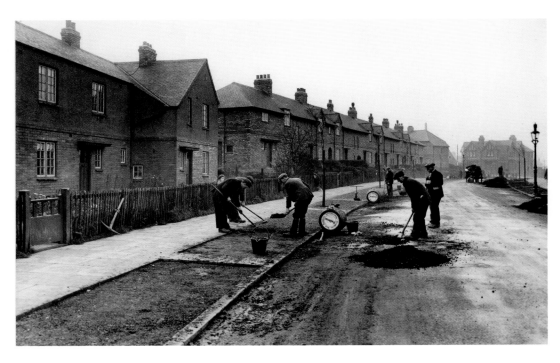

Laying the Turf
The construction of Broadway, Sheriff Hill. The grass verges remain, and the trees have grown nicely. At the end of the road can be seen The Three Tuns public house.

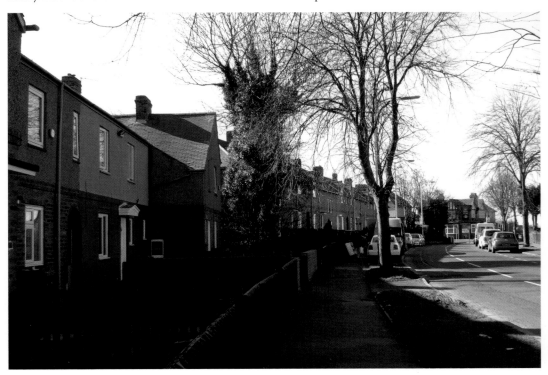

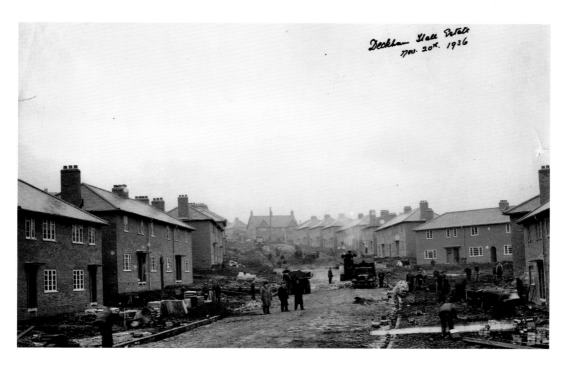

Deckham Hall Estate.
Nov. 20th. 1936

Hendon Road, Deckham

The area of Deckham was named after Sir Thomas Dackham who owned the surrounding land in the early part of the seventeenth century. From the early 1920s all local authorities began council housing programmes and Hendon Road is shown here under construction in November 1936. At the end of the street on Carr Hill Road is the Old Brown Jug public house; it remains, but is now boarded up.

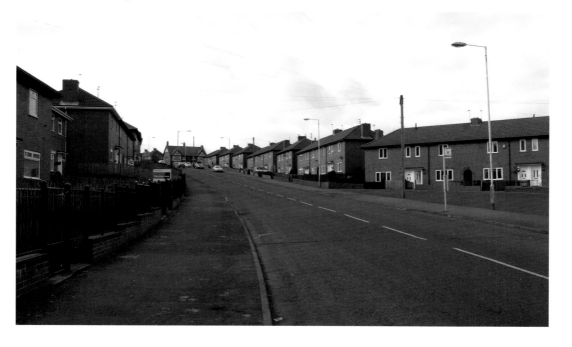

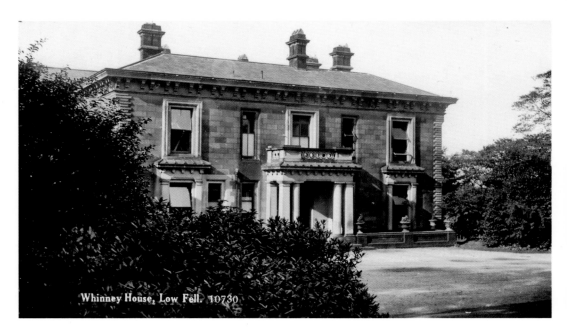

Whinney House, Low Fell. 10730

Whinney House

This was built around 1836 for the Joicey family, and was the largest house built in Low Fell. The most notable member of the family was James Joicey (1846-1936) elected MP for Chester-Le-Street in 1885, holding onto his seat until the election of 1906, then being created the 1st Baron Joicey. Part of the grounds were sold for the construction of Joicey Road Open Air School completed in 1937, and during the war it was used as a military hospital. It has since been used as a nursing home and is currently Gateshead Academy of Torah Studies.

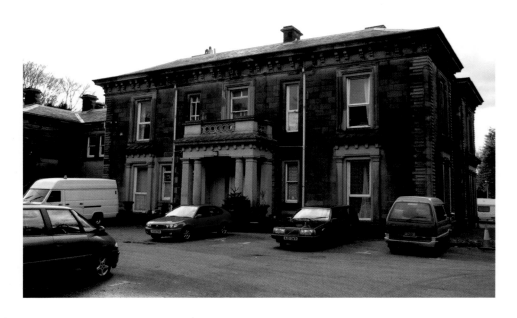

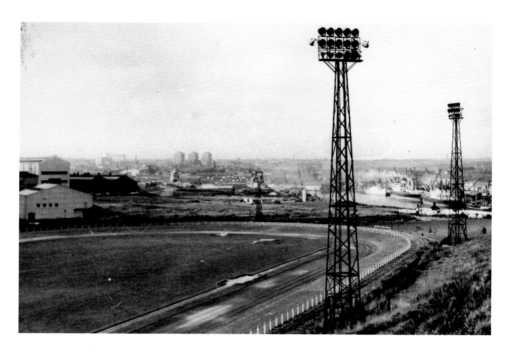

On Your Marks...

Gateshead Stadium *c.* 1960. It was built in 1955 and formally opened by marathon runner Jim Peters on 27 August. Since this photograph was taken numerous improvements have been made (and are still planned) to turn the stadium into an international arena for top-class sporting events – its new name of Gateshead International Stadium reflects its growth in stature. At present it is impossible to recreate this early photograph because the area from where it was taken is in the process of redevelopment.

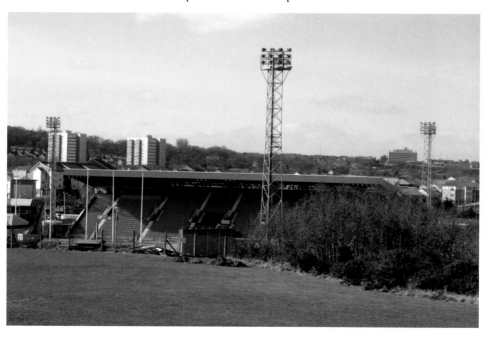

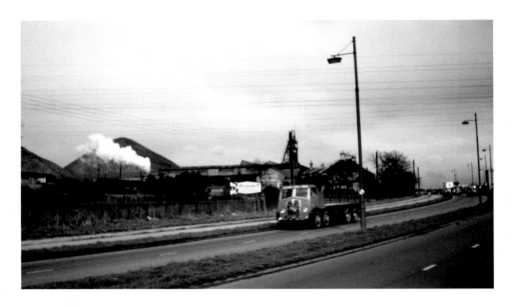

Welcome to Gateshead!

The 'Angel of the North' was commissioned by Gateshead Council and created by Antony Gormley, it is situated just off the busy A1 motorway and is seen by an estimated 33 million people very year. Work started on the sculpture in 1997 and it was assembled in February 1998. It is constructed from 200 tonnes of weathering steel, stands 65ft (20 metres) tall with a wingspan of 175 ft (54 metres), almost the same as a jumbo jet. It stands on a mound created by the closure of the Team Colliery. It was initially viewed with dislike by the nearby residents, but has come to be seen as a positive symbol of Gateshead's regeneration.

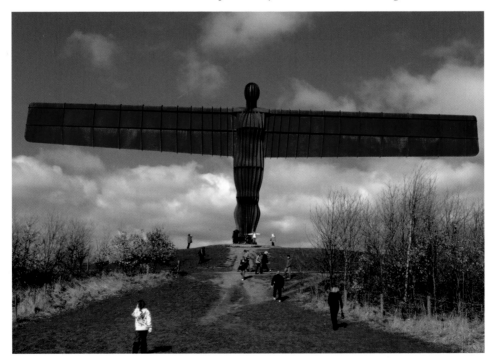